**I Would Like to Dedicate This Book to
Mom and Dad**

Thank You for everything

Leadership Lessons from a Chef

Finding Time to Be Great

Charles M. Carroll

WILEY

John Wiley & Sons, Inc.

All photos by Alex Voigt.

This book is printed on acid-free paper. ∞

Published by John Wiley & Sons, Inc., Hoboken, New Jersey
Published simultaneously in Canada

For general information on our other products and services or for technical support, please contact our Customer Care Department within the United States at (800) 762-2974, outside the United States at (317) 572-3993 or fax (317) 572-4002.

Wiley also publishes its books in a variety of electronic formats. Some content that appears in print may not be available in electronic books. For more information about Wiley products, visit our web site at www.wiley.com.

Library of Congress Cataloging-in-Publication Data:
Carroll, Charles, 1964–.
   Leadership lessons from a chef: finding time to be great / Charles Carroll.
      p. cm.
   Includes index.
   ISBN: 978-0-470-12530-4 (pbk.)
   1. Food service management. 2. Food service—Vocational guidance. I. Title.

TX911.3.M27C365 2007
647.95068—dc22

                                             2006102170

Printed in the United States of America

10

Contents

Foreword

Well, thank God! Someone has finally done it. A book, a bible, a life's journal shared by a real chef in today's modern kitchen. Oh certainly I, as most of you, have read volumes on the subjects of management, team building, communication, and other aspects of managing our environment and teaching others under our jurisdiction to be great at their daily tasks. However, in my thirty years as a chef and culinary CEO, never have I seen a book on this subject written by an executive chef about the realities and challenges facing us in our day-to-day activities.

It became apparent to me that most executive chefs, regardless of stature, receive our education in management from the school of hard knocks. It is pretty much determined for us by most culinary schools or educational facilities that our role as cooks is to cook and it is only through our on-the-job training that we eventually garner the skills necessary to run a successful workplace. What a shame that this antiquated thought process is still considered to be the norm even in the twenty-first century. Today's chefs manage a different workplace. Our kitchens look more like modern food laboratories, staffed with employees ranging from entry level to those with MBAs, multinational to homegrown, with religious preferences and ethnic diversity previously seen only at the United Nations. Today's chefs are asked to not only plan our menus and deliver great visual appeal to the table, but also to communicate company mission, direct sanitation and nutrition classes, understand world flavors and ingredients and in our "spare time" inspire our team to be motivated and innovative day in and day out. Imagine, all of this without formal management training and no one in the wings to give us the support needed to get us through the day.

Well, Chef Charles Carroll has answered our prayers and delivered a masterful text to our desktops. Now it is up to us to open it, read it and put into practice the SEF principle (**S**chedule, **E**mpower, **F**ollow Up!) that Chef Carroll prescribes. Through this practice, you will come to understand how great chefs fail because they lack people skills first and basic managerial ability second. You'll come to embrace what one of America's best chefs has generously shared from his twenty years of practical, out-of-the-box thinking and experience.

I have personally known Chef Carroll for over fifteen years and he has impressed me more and more each year. He is a strategic thinker, the epitome of "planning the work while working the plan." It does not surprise me that it is he who has taken the task upon himself to share with us life's little secret for a successful, professional kitchen driven by a team of committed staff members who "get it." In addition, Chef Carroll continues to drop little gems of wisdom that should be evident to all of us, but through the smoke and heat of the kitchen are often missed or ignored. You will also come to see quickly that there's no theory here; it is fundamentals put into practice and the result shared in a way that's never been told before. As an added bonus, once you've read it, the book becomes your personal handbook for success. It will prove to be a piece as important in your office as **Escoffier's Cookbook, Herring's Dictionary,** or **Larousse's Gastronomique.** In addition, it is the perfect gift to your young apprentices or line cooks, or better yet, to present to a member of your staff who has just endured a reprimand. It reinforces the message that "I care enough about you to give you the tools necessary to learn from your experiences."

Chef Carroll states in this book that "Not everyone can be great, but everyone certainly can be better," and you will, too, if you only choose to follow the commonsense practices outlined in the piece you now hold in your hand. Congratulations, Charles, for a job well done.

Now, read and grow!

Chef John D. Folse, CEC, AAC

Preface

Why is it hard to find an inspirational and motivational book written by a chef for chefs that has tons of practical ideas to use in real kitchens? Are chefs too crazy or too stressed out? Do they just not have enough time? I have always found it frustrating that there are few resources for chefs and culinarians to use to improve themselves or establish positive kitchen environments. For those reasons, I decided to share my thoughts with you.

Okay, let's get one thing straight. I do not have a PhD, a master's degree, or any other title to indicate there is a ten-year college education behind my name. I am a chef with an associate degree from the Culinary Institute of America. I am not going to show you bar graphs, PowerPoint® slideshows, scales, pie charts, or even market studies. You are not going to have to run to get a dictionary to look up big words; but if you do, that means that I had to as well, so it is only fair that you do the same. There are thousands of books out there if you want that kind of read.

Leadership Lessons from a Chef will be worth your salary by the time you are done reading it, and I will tell you why. In the past twelve years, the culinary industry has flourished and acknowledged the chef and compensated him or her accordingly. There are many reasons for this. The chef today is much more visible, more frequently in the dining rooms, managing and dealing with the members (of clubs) and guests on a regular basis, strongly involved with the growth of the property itself—not just concerned with the kitchen. We have celebrity chefs, Iron Chefs, reality chefs, star chefs, personal chefs, White House chefs, and Olympic chefs. America loves cooking shows and follows cooking in the newspapers and on television and radio. Chefs are now in the "front row," when in years past you might never see the chef who cooked your meal. With all these outlets comes a lot of responsibilities. It is no longer only about the food! Chefs are (and will continue to be) expected to be more team leaders and culinary managers than chefs.

In the past twelve years, salaries for chefs have changed dramatically. More and more great positions are opening up with fantastic financial packages. Take a close look at these jobs. What do you see? Why is the chef getting paid better today? More is asked of the chef, more responsibilities, more team building, more management, more front-of-the-house contact. So how are you going to handle this? What in your background is so special that it will allow you to compete for these jobs? What kind of culinary management and team-building background do you have? The chef who is able to build a team and then lead and inspire that team is the chef of today and the future.

This is where our culinary field is weak. For most of us, a few weeks is all we have for management instruction within our formal culinary education. Think about it—a two-year culinary program often offers one class that everyone hates and cannot wait to get out of; it usually occurs during the first semester. Students just want to pass it, get on with it, so they can get into the kitchen and cook. Am I right? As a young person, all this management stuff does not really make sense and seems foreign. They are thinking it will be light years before they will need to manage anyone. Besides, what is most important is how you prepare food, right? Everything else takes a back seat. How do chefs today excel, move up the ranks, and become executive chefs and managers? Well, they go to school, get line-cook jobs, work hard, get promoted to grill chefs, sous chefs, and then one day they become executive chefs. Wait a minute? What happened to the management part? The chef might think: *What did they tell me during those three weeks I was in school?...let me think. Communication, listening skills, inventory, harassment, employee reviews,...ah, I don't remember.* This is one of the reasons, I think, our field is so far behind. Other professions go to school for four years and take dozens of management courses, sometimes before they even know what is their selected field. Granted, culinary bachelor's programs are now popping up more and more at culinary schools, which is a huge step in the right direction. It is a must for all young people entering the culinary field today.

> **"I knew someone had to take the first step, and I made up my mind not to move."**
>
> **—Rosa Parks**

So, having said all that, this book, I promise, will point you in the right direction. This book is better than your management class, because it is based on real kitchen experience. It is quick, to the point, and *real*. There are a lot of great chefs in our industry who are incredible cooks; but they will never excel today at a major property because their people skills—their front-of-the-house polish and their ability to build great teams, to be a leader, to manage and deal with customers, guests, and members on a daily basis— do not exist! That should scare the heck out of you! That's the reason I wrote this book and why I believe it will be one of the best tools you will ever have.

My mission in writing **Leadership Lessons from a Chef** is to inspire you to be great, to inspire you to go the extra mile, to inspire you to use some or all of the ideas in this book and to adapt them for your own operation, whether it be a kitchen, a warehouse, or an office. This book presents a program to help you to build a great team. This book gives you the tools to inspire your team to develop a mission statement for your kitchen, to write the guiding principles by which your team will live, to develop incentive programs, and to find ways to inspire your staff and help them to realize their own goals.

You will read some great ideas in this book, and it is my hope that once you have all the information, you will commit the time to develop your own program. You are being given the gift of the lessons I have learned over twenty years of being an executive chef. It is not brain surgery, just a matter of thinking outside of the box. You have to *find the time to be great!* The secret is scheduling, empowering, and following up. Here is where I give you some brilliant formula studied by management gurus for decades. Actually, this formula is something I came up with on my own: **S**cheduling, **E**mpowering, and **F**ollowing Up, or SEF. Isn't that brilliant? Believe it or not, it can be that simple.

In this book, you will find scores of practical ideas that you can use. Providing good, solid ideas that you can immediately start using pleases me. What I look for every day is something solid, something I can get my arms around, something that allows me to make an intelligent decision and to move forward. If I am successful with my ideas in this book, you should be able to get your arms around a bunch of ideas. You are reading a book written by a chef who works in a lively and incredibly busy country club. These programs are currently in operation at the River Oaks Country Club in Houston, Texas. Is it the "best" kitchen program in the United States? I don't know. Can it be better? Absolutely. Does it work? You better believe it does! That is what drives me. No one showed me how to build it; no one told me that this is how I should do it. I looked for a guide, but I could not find a book written by an experienced chef that discussed how to be a good chef manager. That aspect is what makes this book so exciting for me.

It is my hope that you keep this book handy in your office. I also hope that you will refer to my book when you need a reliable guide or a useful form that will make your job easier. In my opinion, the culinary team-building concepts found in this book could change the way we build our culinary teams, policies, and procedures in the future. Think about it. You start a brand new job today. What steps are you going to take to build your team? What tools do you have to help you create your culinary mission statement, your guiding principles, and your leadership team? Better yet, what culinary team-building book do you have that shows you how to get the most out of your staff and your leadership team? Sure, we have cookbooks; we understand the brigade system; we know how to set up our garde-manger and saucier stations. But how do we get our staff vested into this powerful culinary team? How do we inspire our staff to want to do more? I'm going to help you with all of these questions.

You are reading about all my trials and errors. Real-life stuff, not some hard to believe Fortune 500 company with trillions of dollars to train their employees. I am not going to tell you inspirational stories with warm, fuzzy endings. By the time you get back to your kitchen, you will have forgotten them. I'm going to give you real-life, practical ideas for you to start using today. This book is written by a chef. If I can do it, you can, too. If you can get one thing out of this book that improves your operation or way of life, I will be very happy indeed. I have read many books on team building, and many of them are great books. The problem is that you go back to work with no solid "programs" to put in place, just a bunch of theories. That is what makes this book special. If you are a student, you are reading this at a great time, as you can start these practices now and hit the ground running when it is your turn to supervise or lead a team. Share it with your current chefs, they will be grateful. If you are a chef in charge of a kitchen, now is your time to be great!

One last thing. Yes, these programs do take time; but if you are like me, you thrive on this stuff. SEF: Schedule it, Empower your employees, and Follow up. These concepts are the tools we are going to use. All you need is some direction.

> **"Talent is cheaper than table salt. What separates the talented individuals from the successful one is a lot of hard work."**
>
> **—Stephen King**

We have a program in our catering office that I created to help sell our functions to the members. It is an awesome program, with over 600 digital images that I will talk about in more detail later in the book. We have been using this program since 2002; four years later, I still cannot find anyone else doing this. I asked my boss one day, I wonder why nobody else has adopted this program? I have toured hundreds of people through the system. He said, "I know why, Charles. It is too much work." It increases sales, blows away the members, and improves consistency in the kitchen. What more do you want? The moral of this story is—if it were easy, everybody would be doing it! The concepts in this book are simple ones, but that does not necessarily mean they are *easy* to implement. They require commitment and perseverance. Not everyone can be great, but most can be better than they are. You are getting this information right off the line!

Let's get started.

Acknowledgments

Many times I have said how blessed my career has been. I have many people to thank for that, people who allowed me to make my mistakes, learn from them, and grow.

I would like to thank Chef Phil Learned, CEC, AAC, and the Balsams Grand Resort Hotel in Dixville Notch, New Hampshire; both had faith in me at a very young age.

Many thanks to the entire 1988 New England Culinary Olympic Team, which took me under its wing at a young age and trained me to Olympic form. Also, to all Olympic teams that followed, many, many thanks for all you have taught me. Chef Keith Keogh, CEC, AAC; Chef Edward Leonard, CMC, AAC; and the American Culinary Federation—thank you for giving me the dream of representing the United States in the World Culinary arena.

To fond memories with Chef Noel Cullen, CMC, thank you for the many leadership lessons. I know you have been watching from above, as I grasp for my thoughts and find a way to get them on paper.

I am also grateful to Eric Rule, general manager, and Oak Hill Country Club in Rochester, New York. Eric is a great friend and a fantastic boss who mentored me at my first country club position.

A special thank you to Chef John Folse, CEC, AAC, for being a great friend, an inspirational leader, and always taking time out for me. *"Look John, I finally did it!"*

To Dwight Edwards, who has been a great influence on my perspective on life and who is an incredible talent and resource for River Oaks Country Club.

To General Manager Joe Bendy of River Oaks Country Club. Truly an inspirational leader, a fantastic boss, and a special friend. Joe has an incredible perspective on managing people, and I have learned a great deal from him.

Many thanks to Chef Gary Eaton, who spent many hours tearing up the book and providing great insight on how to put it back together. Thanks for taking a personal interest in the project.

To Chef Tommy Vaccaro, CEPC, dear friend, teammate, colleague, and dangerous golfing partner. Tommy, thanks for bending over backward to help me present these concepts at conventions. The amount of work you did for me is truly admirable, and I thank you for your support.

A very special and heartfelt thank you to River Oaks Country Club Culinary Leadership Team: Timothy Prefontaine, CSC; Darrin Aoyama, CEPC; Paul Williams, CEC; Kevin Bayer; Antonio Franco; Elaina Deloya; Michael Owens; Adam Heath; Evan De Long; Jesus Lopez; and my assistant Maria Canlas. This team was a big part of this book, and they are a great inspiration to me. Thank you!

Thank you to Ben E. Keith, and Ron Boyd, Senior Vice President, for all of their support and great service.

Many thanks to the Wiley family: Melissa Oliver, who had faith in the project, and a big thanks to Julie Kerr, senior developmental editor, who was absolutely a pleasure to work with.

And finally, a very special thanks to my incredibly supportive wife Torill, who not only gave me great feedback on the book but also tolerated all of the hours that were needed to produce it. Torill and daughters Kelsey and Randi have been very patient and understanding my whole career and for that I thank them.

About the Author

Chef Charles M. Carroll is currently the executive chef of River Oaks Country Club, Houston, Texas, one of the top five country clubs in the United States. From 1996 through 2000, he was executive chef at Oak Hill Country Club, home of the Ryder Cup, the U.S. Amateur, U.S. Open, U.S. Senior Open, and the PGA golf championships. He also served as the executive chef at the Balsams Grand Resort Hotel, a four-star, four-diamond resort located in Dixville Notch, New Hampshire, for thirteen years.

Chef Carroll's presentations have inspired professionals all over the United States and in Europe. His contemporary style comprises culinary demonstrations; building leadership and culinary policies and procedures programs; and team-building seminars. His expertise is highly sought after.

A 1985 graduate of the Culinary Institute of America, Chef Carroll will also serve as a coach for the 2008 U.S. Culinary Olympic National Team, his seventh Olympic team. He has served as a coach, manager, or competitor on six previous Culinary Olympic teams, winning more than seventy national and international awards.

Other awards Chef Carroll has received include Chef of the Year and Educator of the Year from the American Culinary Federation (ACF) and three American Culinary Foundation President's medallions. He has been inducted into the World Master Chefs Association, the American Academy of Chefs, the Confrérie de la Chaîne des Rôtisseurs, and the Honorable Order of the Golden Toque. Chef Carroll serves as president to the Board of Trustees of the LeNotre Culinary Institute and as secretary treasurer of Les Amis d'Éscoffier Society Houston.

Chapter 1

What Makes You Tick?

W hat makes this book realistic about "team building" but useful and still fun is that most of what is required is raw material—hard work, sweat, trial-and-error—that comes from the heart. I'm not going to tell you hypothetical stories about two mice or moving mountains. What most motivates me about food is what I still have to learn. What most inspires me is working with young professionals and building great teams. From day one, building great teams has been something I have thrived on; I love building a culinary team in the same way that a pro football coach builds a team. I work hard to find the perfect fit for each position—the perfect chef, journeyman, or student—for the perfect position. I have sometimes moved chefs to different positions to maximize their strengths or to maximize the team's depth, just as a football coach would. It is really that simple. Do you ever review your team and then move the chefs around so they don't get stagnant? Do you ever wonder if your team would be stronger if you made some of these moves?

Sometimes the Best Solution Is Right in Front of You

> **"What most inspires me is working with young professionals and building great teams."**

I remember I needed a garde-manger chef and could not find the right person for the job. It was a difficult position that needed someone who could think on his or her feet, who was able to make decisions, and who could supervise a staff of ten, not to mention possessing the garde-manger skills required for the position. In the midst of my frustration, an apprentice came to me and asked, "Why don't you promote your wife to the position?" Now, first off, working with your wife in the same building, let alone the same kitchen, isn't always a good idea; but in this case it was a great idea. My wife is a no-nonsense Norwegian chef who trained with a two-star Michelin chef. On my best day I have a trace of nonsense in me, so why she married me is still a mystery. Anyway, the apprentice was right. I had the best person for the job already in my kitchen; but because I did not look outside the box, I could not see it. This is really important in your operation. You need to take a good look around, often, to see if there is a move that would benefit both the chef and the company. Some of the best moves may not be the obvious ones.

> 1. Consider those around you for key roles in your team.
> 2. Be willing to take risks.
> 3. Just because it isn't obvious does not mean it is not a good idea.
> 4. Step outside the situation and look at the challenge as a whole.

Early Influences

It all started for me at Rabbit Hill Inn in Waterford, Vermont. My mother, Ruth, and father, John, bought the Inn in 1972 when I was eight years old. Even so young, I had to work my tail off several days a week. Those of you who have grown up in a family business or who are familiar with owning your own business know it is an eight-day-a-week job. I had regular chores that included stocking bars, running for ice, showing guests to their rooms, setting up fireplaces—you name it, I had to do it. I actually worked the breakfast station when I was ten years old. What I did not realize until later in life, however, was that growing up in this environment was very special, and my experience later benefited my career tremendously. Not only did I grow up in an incredibly disciplined environment, my home constantly had guests. Brothers Greg and Tom, sister Celinda, and I were constantly on stage, as it were. We could not throw fits, fight over toys, toss food at the table (okay, there was this one time...never mind), or fight over the remote (well, there was no remote, and we only had two channels). My point is that we were always busy taking care of guests; when we were not taking care of them, the guests could see us. I think this made us grow up faster.

> **"One of the marks of true greatness is the ability to develop greatness in others."**
>
> **—J. C. McCauley**

Most important of all, I learned: how to behave in front of people, not to be afraid to talk to people, and proper manners. I did not realize how important this was until I saw other chefs afraid to walk into the dining room to talk with their guests. Some chefs are so nervous about giving a demonstration that it would prevent them from sleeping the night before or cause them to throw up just before the presentation. I did not realize what an effect this early prep had on me. Growing up in this environment was special, a lot of work, but special. My early first-hand experiences unknowingly paved the way for my professional career.

My Early Profession

My next position was at the Balsams Grand Resort, a 15,000-acre, four-star, four-diamond resort in the northern tip of New Hampshire. I apprenticed there, went to the Culinary Institute of America, graduated, and returned to the resort, supposedly long enough to get some money in my pocket and to research my first big job. Little did I know that that *was* my first big job. Working there for two years prior to beginning my formal culinary education and making my way through every department, made it easy to go back. I was able to rise very quickly from sous chef to apprenticeship coordinator to executive sous chef and finally to executive chef by age 24.

> **"The beauty about my passion is that to this day, I have not stopped working to improve my qualifications."**

I had sixty employees working for me in the kitchen, more than half of whom were older than me. It was a pretty challenging task, although at the time I didn't think so. I would have chewed off the end of a wooden table if that is what it took to be successful. In many ways, working with the resort's apprenticeship program made me realize early on the significance and mechanics of building a great team. The apprentices believed in me, which in turn put a lot of pressure on me. It made me want to be better and to have all the answers. I remember someone telling my boss at the Balsams that I was not old enough or qualified enough for the executive chef job at the age of 24. Think about that statement for a moment. Talk about providing motivation and inspiration!

> **"People don't care how much you know, until they know how much you care."**
>
> **—John C. Maxwell**

What better motivation could you have than someone telling your boss that you are not ready for the job or that you are not qualified! I might have agreed with him to a point, but the beauty about my passion is that to this day I have not stopped working to improve my qualifications. All my life I have had "young" kitchens and a refreshingly hungry kitchen atmosphere. What the team lacked in experience, we usually made up in effort and will— and a "chewing off the end of the table" mentality. I love that!

1. Turn challenges into motivations.
2. Always work twice as hard as those around you to enhance and improve your qualifications.
3. Don't be afraid of what you do know, and don't be afraid of what you don't know.
4. Realize that you never have all the answers, rely on the talent that surrounds you.
5. Ask the opinions of those around you.
6. Agree as a team once the team has come to a conclusion.
7. If you show your staff that you are genuinely interested in their opinion, they will respect you.

Wearing the Right Shoes

A friend of mine once told me that you have to pretend to be something before you can actually become it. Think about it. You cannot just flip a switch and be an executive chef one day. I practiced every day until I was confident that I knew every department just as well as the department head. You have to practice and put yourself in the shoes of the chef every day. Don't put blinders on and worry only about the task at hand. Learn about everything that goes on around you. It kills me when I have a cook who thinks he or she is ready for a sous chef position and don't even know what time the dinner function is going out that night or even what the menu is, for that matter. As a new professional you should be eager, and you should want to excel and take the next step. But don't lose track of the concept that you need to *LEARN* first. You can't get so wrapped up in getting your name on your chef's jacket and the department head black pants. In fact, I tell my superstars to be patient, and chances are they will fly by many of the chefs who have mentored them. But patience is the key. The most important thing in your career as a new professional is to train well and work hard, work harder than anybody around you. If you do that, trust me, you will be great.

> **"Focus on your work, not the titles. If you produce beyond expectations, the titles will come."**

Let me tell you a secret for new professionals. Show up! What I mean by show up is just that: Show up ready! Do you know how many average-to-below-average employees we see day after day, week after week, year after year? Do you have any idea how wearing that is? More employees are concerned with when they get out rather than what they can get out of the experience, more concerned with how tired they are than how much more energy they have. Some employees are worried that someone else in the kitchen is actually doing less work than they are.

Show Up!

This is the secret. If you show up to work focused and prepared for the day and work harder than anybody around you, the executive chef will notice. The chef will give you more responsibilities; you will move to the top of the promotion list because you have made a choice to do the job and to do it to the best of your abilities.

Do not give the chef any other option but to recognize you. Just do it! Believe it or not, it takes as much energy to do a great job as it does to do a poor job. So why not be great, do great? Trust me, you will feel better doing a great day of work as opposed to cheating yourself through the day.

Arriving in the kitchen ready to work sets the tone for the rest of the chefs.

1. Train well.
2. Work hard.
3. Work harder.

Mentoring

"YOU have the power to make a difference in the lives of everyone you touch. That is pretty special."

Chef John Folse is a dear friend of mine and a great inspiration to me. At last count, he has thirteen companies, all built by him. I have known John for fifteen years, and he is a true genius. He is one of the busiest chefs I know, a make-it-happen kind of guy, in case you haven't been able to figure that out. One thing that is very special about John is that he always has time for me. As busy as he is, with all his companies, TV shows, radio shows, and culinary classes, he always takes my calls. I've been bugging him for years with half-cocked ideas, and he always finds ways to put me on the right path. This is very special to me and a good lesson for all of us. Don't start getting wrapped up in your own press such that you forget to stop and help those just beginning their culinary careers. That has to be one of the best benefits of our job, helping young people. YOU have the power to make a difference in the lives of everyone you touch. That is pretty special.

When John first started his cheese company, he told me he was going to find the best cheese maker he could find, hire him, and then learn more about cheese making than the cheese maker himself. And that is what he did! You can't be afraid to surround yourself with talented people, especially those more talented than you. John has a weekly meeting with all his managers from all his properties. They *all* give their reports; John gives them *all* direction and lets them run their departments. He empowers them to do the right thing.

Seek out challenges and work toward learning from them and ultimately conquering them. Do the research needed to be great. Have you ever heard the saying, "Sometimes I think it is good to put the cart in front of the horse; this will make you work harder." Sometimes I book several deadlines in a short time period just to keep myself motivated and focused and to keep the pressure on.

Has anybody ever asked something of you, to run a demonstration, to give a lecture, to assist in a competition or a special event? It would be fun once you got there, but the road getting there was going to be a boatload of work? Great opportunities don't usually come to those people who choose to sit on their hands. Great opportunities come to those who work hard. What I mean by booking several events or deadlines to keep focused is that if you tell somebody you're going to do something, if you agree to an assignment, put an event in writing, it's now up to you to do it! You own it. Therefore, you have to be careful about what you agree to do. I choose the events that I know I will benefit from in the long run as a professional or those that I know will make a huge influence on someone's career.

Question Yourself, Question Your Team

There is a simple exercise I learned from Chef Ferdinand Metz, CMC. If you are not satisfied with something, ask yourself some questions. Sounds easy, but do you do it? Or do you just let it slide, because it is good enough?

Consider this. Let us say you are plating a banquet, the first plate comes off the line and you don't like it for some reason. The food is fine—servable but not stellar. What is not right about it? Ask yourself some questions. *What don't you like about it? Is the color okay? How about the textures, doneness, portions?* You can start a whole series of questions until you find the answers you need to be great. Imagine this menu: pan-seared Chilean sea bass with mashed potatoes and broccoli. There is a lot of room for improvement here, but where do you start?

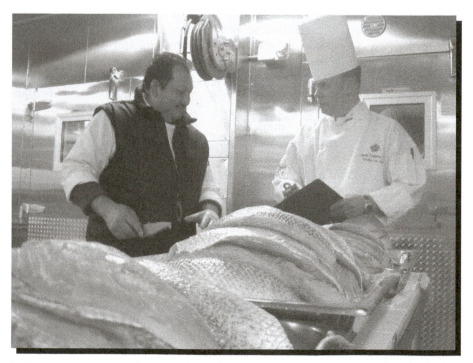

Asking questions is a first step in making sure the quality you want is achieved.

"If you are not a team, you're just a crowd of people standing in an empty room."

Some of the questions I would ask include the following:

- Do I like the way the plate looks?
  No.
- What don't I like about the look of the plate?
  Very plain looking, white fish, white potatoes, green vegetable. The plate is too elementary looking.
- Do I like the components and the composition of the plate?
  I like Chilean sea bass, but I don't like how the potato and the broccoli go with it.
- What kind of vegetable and starch would I like to see on the plate? How can I make the plate look better while adding components that are compatible with the sea bass?
  I would like to see better color, maybe a broiled, marinated tomato, maybe some spinach and arugula sautéed with prosciutto.
- What do I want to see for sauce and starch? Is this for lunch or dinner?
  I think for lunch I would keep it lighter, maybe some lightly saffron-poached pearl couscous tossed in with the spinach. Yellow pepper coulis would taste great with all of the ingredients and look great with the tomato and spinach.
- How does it all come together?
  Coriander-dusted Chilean sea bass atop wilted arugula, spinach, and prosciutto, broiled vine-ripened tomato, and yellow pepper coulis.

You can use this concept with any subject. You just have to be smart enough, or brave enough, to ask the questions until you get to the bottom of the problem. This really is a great tool, and it works not just with the food you prepare but with the people who work for you.

How Is Your Team?

Always question how things are going and what can be improved. Here are eight great questions to ask yourself to make sure your team is on the right path:

1. Do you have a great team?
2. Is your team inspired?

> 3. Is your team motivated?
> 4. Are you motivated and if not, why not?
> 5. How do you rate the atmosphere in your kitchen? Is it a fun and productive kitchen?
> 6. Do your employees enjoy working for you?
> 7. Do your employees follow your lead?
> 8. How often do you lose your temper or raise your voice in your kitchen?

"To do a common thing, uncommonly well, brings success."

—Henry Heinz

Motivate Your Team Members

Meet Jack, who works in the early morning. Jack has been late several times and has received verbal and written warnings. He has been given extra chances by the banquet sous chef to perform his duties on time. Finally, the executive sous chef came to me and said that Jack needed to be fired. He can't seem to get through to Jack that he needs to be on time. Jack claims he has three alarm clocks but sleeps right through them. He just hates working in the morning and hates getting up early. Now, I always thought Jack was a pretty good guy. I even sent him to another property to train during our slow time. He had really set himself up to be fired, but I wanted to get into his head a little, so I decided to bring him in my office to have a "sit-down." This is basically how it went:

"Jack, you're having a difficult time getting to work on time."

"Yes sir."

"What seems to be the problem?"

"I don't know Chef, it's not like I'm partying or staying out late, you can ask the guys. I just can't get up on time. Can't you move me? I asked to be moved to another P.M. station a month ago, but my request was ignored."

"First, Jack, normally we move our staff during the off seasons. And, second, we like to reward great performances. It appears that yours has been less than stellar."

"I just hate the breakfast and lunch banquets."

"The first rule of holes: When you're in one, stop digging."

—Molly Ivins, columnist

It kills me when I have a young and sometimes cocky student, journeyman, or cook in my office, and they tell me how they don't want to work pantry, breakfast station, or banquets. I try to keep my cool as I talk to them. It is my job to help point out the importance of our industry and all the elements that go with it. This is key. As a new professional, you don't see all the potential a property has that can possibly help catapult you into culinary success. Think back to when you were just beginning in this field, and imagine the impact an advisor or mentor had on you. If you didn't have anyone to help shepherd your career, think about how awesome it would have been to receive advice from someone experienced. Regardless of your own experience, it is now your job—you are the coach, the advisor—you can make a difference in a person's life. They may not always recognize it, but someday they will understand that you helped them tremendously. This is very special. Okay, let's get back to Jack.

"Let me ask you something, do you anticipate staying in the culinary field?" A bold question; but sometimes such questions bring surprising answers. You need to find out what your employee is thinking.

Jack, looking astonished that I even asked such a question, answered: "Of course, Chef, this is my life!"

"Where do you see your first executive chef position being?"

Jack's eyes started to open wider. "Well, I'm not sure yet, but I want to see the country and find out. Maybe a club or a resort or restaurant."

You could see the excitement in his expression.

"Well that's a good start, Jack. Do you foresee not serving breakfast or lunch at any of these properties?"

Jack's face went blank, as he started to turn red.

"I suppose they will serve lunch and breakfast but..."

I then ask, getting in his face a little, "What is the recipe for the beautiful, fresh ginger pancake batter you picked up from the bakeshop this morning? Or what about the raisin bread for the French toast? What about the club's signature sticky buns? I just love them, don't you? Do you have those recipes?"

Jack is starting not to feel so well. "Well, no, Chef, no, I don't," he said.

"Seems to me they would be good recipes to have as you're touring the country looking for the first executive chef position, would you agree? What about your station, do you know how many cases of eggs it takes to feed 100 people? Bacon? Potatoes? Do you have all our soup recipes? Or, better yet, do you know what soups we are serving at the club today? Are you going to buy all your salad dressings at your fancy restaurant?"

> "Success seems to be connected with action. Successful people keep moving. They make mistakes, but they don't quit."
> —Conrad Hilton, hotel executive

In my opinion, breakfast, in many properties, is not done very well. There is an art to breakfast preparation and something special about a breakfast done well and with passion. The bottom line is that we have to point these things out to many new professionals. Tutor them; make sure they are building their resources. Your A players will already be doing this, but you need to be sure you are pushing your B players as well.

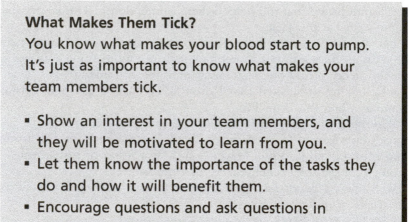

What Makes Them Tick?
You know what makes your blood start to pump. It's just as important to know what makes your team members tick.

- Show an interest in your team members, and they will be motivated to learn from you.
- Let them know the importance of the tasks they do and how it will benefit them.
- Encourage questions and ask questions in return.

So Jack finally started to get the point. I suggested to him that he should be building an incredible resource book for every department he is in. And if I were a new chef, just getting started, I would be getting into the bakeshop as well, to get all the experience possible, so when I'm running the kitchen, I would be able to explain to my crew exactly what I needed. Everything Jack needs to be a successful executive chef is right in front of him. As leaders we have to help point out all of the opportunities to our staff. Help them *see,* give them guidance. Long story short, Jack did finish his season on the morning banquets, and we moved him to P.M. à la cart, and he is doing great! He is a lot happier and has not been late yet. His whole attitude has changed. Maybe we made a difference in this young man's life. It would be great if we did!

What many young people don't understand is that moving them from department to department does not necessarily benefit the company, at least, not early on. It takes a lot of hard work, preparation, and planning by everyone involved, just to make this chef a better culinarian. Sure it would be much easier to leave the chefs in the departments in which they are most talented—less stress and no transitional errors or slowdowns. But what does that do to your staff? Do they get stagnant, bored? Do they feel they need to go to another property in order to grow? Sure, it is more difficult to move young staff from department to department, but in the end your staff will be strong and versatile, and they will understand each other's jobs—it becomes a stronger team. As executive chef, this is our investment and, trust me, your return will be well worth it.

Chapter 2

Testing the Kitchen Atmosphere

I am going to ask what is hopefully a stupid question for you: Do your chefs taste everything before they serve it? It is crazy to me that once in a while I still catch chefs putting out food without having tasted it first. Mostly, because they are just pumping out the food, they don't stop to taste.

One day I had a chef make fifteen gallons of spaghetti sauce for a children's luncheon to be held the following day. The next morning he heated up the sauce and started serving the party. I came over and tasted the sauce; it was scorched. I held the tasting spoon up and asked, "Did you taste this sauce?" I was a little upset, because I always preach, "Taste everything." In fact, it is one of our guiding principles, which I am going to talk about later. He said, "I tasted it yesterday, Chef."

"Yeah, and you burnt it today!" I said.

We have to continue to cook, no matter how busy we are; but I insist that everyone taste everything.

Stop and Smell the Roses (or the Roast)

I can just about tell when a prime rib is ready after slow roasting in the oven. You can smell the caramelization in the air. You can smell the fat rendering and self basting this beautiful piece of meat. We know we have to start out roasting the prime rib at a high temperature until you can start to hear the meat sizzle, lock in the juices, then turn down the temperature, and cook the meat slowly on low heat. This perfect roasting technique allows the meat to cook perfectly, end to end. There is nothing more beautiful than when you slice a prime rib or a rack of lamb, after the meat has rested properly, and it is perfectly done and consistent from the top of the slice to the bottom.

The reason I'm spending so much time on this is because I often find that chefs and cooks, believe it or not, don't cook. They are going through motions, as they put the meat in the oven. They neither massage the temperature nor monitor the meat and aroma during the process; then they take the meat out of the oven, sometimes putting the roast in areas that are too hot, so the meat overcooks. Or, they will not plan the timing of the roast well enough, and end up slicing the meat immediately rather than letting it rest, and all the juices come running out and the meat looks like a sponge. At this point, you might as well serve me boiled barn owl. Cooking is an art, cooking is passion, your passion is hard at work. The more passionate the cook, the better the flavors. Be careful you don't catch yourself just going through the motions. It can happen to anybody, especially in a very busy property when chefs don't think they have time to use proper techniques. Great cooks handle the beautifully roasted prime rib as if it is their firstborn. Ahh, the smell of beautifully caramelized mirepoix—the carrots, celery, and onion turning perfectly golden brown—that is a happy kitchen!

> **"The more passionate the cook, the better the flavors."**

Know What You Are Serving

1. Taste the food.
2. Taste the food.
3. Taste the food.

Talking Food

Equally important to building a good team and making good food is talking about food. What is the conversation like in your kitchen now? Cooks and chefs like to talk about what happened last night and what they are doing tonight or over the weekend, watercooler conversation, as they say. Inspire them to talk about food. Ask them questions about classic foods. Deliberately spark conversations about food. Now, I can see you sitting there reading this saying: "Yeah that makes sense, yeah that sounds good, what else have you got?" Imagine if all your cooks thrived on culinary conversation! What an atmosphere! Inspire your team to talk about food.

One Thanksgiving we were very busy checking all the turkeys, hams, prime ribs, and legs of lamb. We were crazy busy, with roughly one hundred complete to-go meals and 1,100 for lunch service. The hustle around the kitchen was at a good level. I saw one of the cooks checking the internal temperature of one of the twelve prime ribs. He took the probe out of the rib, wiped it, and placed it in his pocket and then he started to take *all* the ribs out. I asked him what he was doing?

"Taking the ribs out, Chef," he said with a sense of urgency.

"What was the internal temperature of the ribs?"

"120°F, Chef, on the dot, just like you wanted."

"I trust the first one you checked was 120°F; but what about the other eleven that you did not check the temp of?"

The chef stopped in his shoes with a look on his face like, are you really going to make me put all these roasting pans back in the oven? I explain to him all the ribs do not weigh the same and not all of the ovens keep the same heat, so each roast has to be tested. At that point, I asked a younger apprentice what temperature the lamb should be. Then we started talking about the fact that the bigger the piece of meat, the more the temperature will carry over after you take the roast out of the oven. Yet another chef chimed in with the fact that a steamship roast of beef would have to come out of the oven at 110°F internal temperature because the size of the meat causes the steamship temperature to carry over longer. At this point, everyone started quizzing all temperatures of a variety of meat, and everyone was learning.

One time I had a cook who was making some quiche; when he pulled it out of the oven, it was caramelized but not set. You could not slice it. I asked him what was his ratio. He looked at me like I had three heads. "What do you mean?" he asked. "I mean, what is YOUR ratio?" I said.

I could not believe he did not have a ratio for the custard. Granted, there are many different quiche recipes—some with milk, some with cream and milk, some with whole eggs and yolks, and some with just eggs—but all cooks should have a basic custard ratio in their head that they know works, like 7 to 1: 7 eggs to 1 quart of milk is at least a good starting point.

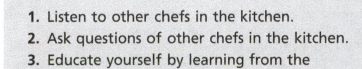

1. Listen to other chefs in the kitchen.
2. Ask questions of other chefs in the kitchen.
3. Educate yourself by learning from the experiences of those you work with.

Talk about food. You will be surprised how many cooks start listening in on your conversation. You will be surprised how many join in the discussion.

Discussions among chefs should be encouraged as part of the learning process.

Most of them want to learn. Next thing you know you're having a whole discussion on ratios. How important is this? I remember a chef at the CIA (Culinary Institute of America) constantly giving us ratios, so by the end of the three-week class we had pages of ratios. These are the special keys to cooking. You can braise any piece of meat, as long as you understand the art of braising. Ratios work on the same principle.

Challenge Your Team; Inspire Your Team

Challenge your team, and they will challenge you back. How about getting everyone involved in an educational conversation about one of Éscoffier's classic recipes? How about one of Éscoffier's famous consommés? It has to start with YOU! How exciting is it to a young chef when you explain the consommé concept and ratio and how it works. I will never need a cookbook to make a consommé. Sure, if I want to research some different flavor profiles or garnish ideas, I can look in cookbooks for that; but my point is that I will always have the perfect ratio in my head. *How the acid works with the albumen. How you have to stir the raft until it reaches 120°F, then stop stirring because that is when egg whites start to coagulate. How the impurities that slowly rise to the top have to be cleared away.* How amazing is that concept? What about the consommé ratio? How special is it when you give a young chef the ratio of 3 egg whites, 1 pound of protein, 1 gallon of stock, and some acid? You can make any consommé you want! This formula will work with any protein. These are the conversations we should be hearing in the kitchen.

All of the lessons that follow in this book start with you. We have to change in order to change others. If the executive chef uses bad language in the kitchen, does not talk about food, and does not challenge the staff, they will not challenge themselves! End of story!

1. Talk
2. Listen
3. Learn
4. Listen some more

The Days of Screaming Chefs Are Over

In years past, much of the kitchen turnover rate was accredited to the atmosphere created by the head chef. There are still kitchens today with chefs who have a reputation for screaming at their staff and working people eighty and ninety hours or more a week. Many new cooks and chefs commit to this environment for a short time just to get the incredible food experience, and then they quit. They can only take the punishment for so long, getting burnt out in the process. People do not want to work in an uncomfortable atmosphere. They do not want to be yelled at, embarrassed, or humiliated.

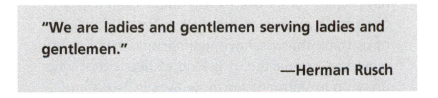

"We are ladies and gentlemen serving ladies and gentlemen."

—Herman Rusch

I live by a three-strike rule. First strike: You make a mistake, I am going to point it out to you. Second strike: I will give you a stern reminder that we already talked about the problem. Third strike: I will lose it, but I rarely raise my voice. Sometimes silence is deadly. More often than not, the good employees will put pressure on themselves.

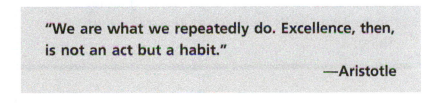

"We are what we repeatedly do. Excellence, then, is not an act but a habit."

—Aristotle

It is funny, I've had three executive chef jobs in seventeen years, and each time my predecessor was a screamer. This made my entry to the new job seem like a great breath of fresh air to the staff. I could almost feel the positive energy coming from the staff. Many years of getting beaten up takes its toll. I can't remember the last time I raised my voice at an employee. Now I didn't say my temper, or my tempo, stayed level, but I did not raise my voice. Usually, when we lose our tempers and raise our voices, it is because we are frustrated, angry, and busy, and sometimes fatigue plays a role. Yelling may make you feel better, get it off your chest, relieve "your" stress, but what about all the stress you just caused in the kitchen? You may have corrected the situation with the chef temporarily, but you haven't solved it in the long term if this is all you are going to do. Stopping the bleeding does not cure the patient.

Body Language

Do you want to get a reality check on your personal body language? Try asking one of your outspoken, nonshy chefs his or her impression of you. You will likely be surprised by what they have to say (don't ask for the impression if you don't have a sense of humor!). I don't think any of us think that we have mannerisms that can be mimicked or enacted. It is kind of like a chef who grew up in Vermont but now lives in Texas and thinks everyone else talks funny while he sounds normal. No one considers their own speech accented, right? My point is that everyone in the kitchen picks up on your body language all day long. So just imagine how you look. One of our guiding principles is a quote from Herman Rusch, "We are ladies and gentleman serving ladies and gentleman." Let's get back to the screaming thing.

Positive Body Language

- Always make eye contact with your team members.
- Say what you mean and mean what you say. Think before you answer.
- Do not slouch. Walk tall.
- Be conscious of your facial expressions; be sure your message does not come across negative.
- Your smile is the most powerful and positive body signal you have.
- Have a firm handshake.

"You may have stopped the bleeding but you have not cured the patient."

Speaking Softly Carries Great Weight

There may be times where your voice will rise or you make a situation personal, causing you to lose your temper, but there are a few things you should think about.

1. Make sure raising your voice or temper is absolutely necessary.
2. If you are addressing a particular employee, do it privately and not on a grandstand in the middle of the kitchen.
3. If you lose your temper in the middle of the kitchen, blasting someone in front of the rest of the staff, you are doing it for your own ego and not for the good of the team.
4. If you "blast" someone, do it sparingly and effectively.
5. Address the issue immediately and not several weeks after the fact.
6. Carefully explain what the problem is and exactly what is expected of the individual in the future.

Your expectations and directions have significant impact on the performance of your staff. Most importantly, reinforce the correct behavior as soon as it happens.

I recently had an instance where I got pretty upset. We had a new employee start working without all the proper paperwork completed. Now, in this day and age, this just cannot happen, does not happen, should not happen...but it happened. This is a cardinal sin at our club. One of my chefs, let us call him Norm, is in charge of all new employee paperwork. There were several reasons this did happen, all very valid reasons: (1) it was a holiday weekend, (2) there was a miscommunication about the appointment with human resources (HR), and (3) Norm was off work the day the new employee was scheduled to start. But, unfortunately, there is no excuse. I got the call from HR and was told the employee was not fully processed. At the same time, Chef Norm got an e-mail stating the same thing. By the time Chef Norm got to my office, my body language must have been pretty clear because before I could say a word, Chef Norm said: "Chef, I'm sorry. It was my fault. It was a misunderstanding, and it will not happen again." I felt like saying, "You bet it won't happen again," but I didn't. Chef Norm knew the severity of the situation, all I needed to do was to run through a series of questions to find out how it happened, review with Norm the expected behavior of the hiring process, and let it go.

> "The most important single ingredient in the formula of success is knowing how to get along with people."
>
> —Theodore Roosevelt

It used to be common practice that when your dog had an accident in the house, you rubbed his nose in it and then put the dog outside. This was supposed to teach him not to do it in the house again. Well, guess what, that scares the dog more than anything and actually the opposite happens. You rub the dog's nose in the mess and then throw him outside, he's thinking, "Every time I have an accident, they rub my nose in it. I better stop doing my business." The poor dog gets all backed up and constipated because he's scared to death. Anyway, the days of screaming and rubbing our staff's noses in their mistakes should be over. It is up to us to lead our staff to success.

Giving your time to your chefs helps to set the tone of your leadership.

We have to be careful how we talk to our staff so we don't send the wrong message.

Stay on Message

What is the message we give our staff? Do you lead by example? Do you set clear and understandable directions, goals, and standards for them? Do they have a clear understanding of what their jobs are? Do you make yourself clear when addressing them? My point goes back to what happens to the dog. He gets scared of the trainer and confused by the instructions.

What happens to those team members you scream at in the middle of the kitchen? Yeah, you feel better; good for you. Are we getting the full potential of that employee? My bet is that you have just shoved any confidence that that person once had so deep into her or his being that you may never see that employee's full potential. Granted the production around this person may have picked up because the staff is scared to death, afraid they are next, but what kind of atmosphere is that to work in? The only sure bet is that you will have a lot of turnover.

Instead, I hope you feel inspired every time one of your team members moves on to the next job. Remember, every person who leaves you is like a customer: They tell ten people, and those ten people each tell ten more, and so on.

How about pulling the employee over to the side to talk. Put your arm on his or her shoulder and say: "Chef, we have talked about this problem a few times now, right?"

"Yes, Chef, we have."

"You understand that I'm starting to get pretty upset by the fact that you are continuing to ignore my instructions. Is there any particular reason we are having a problem communicating?"

"No, Chef, I just dropped the ball. I'm sorry."

"You understand that if this problem comes up again, I am going to have to write you up, and it will go in your file. Do we understand each other? Is there something else I can do to help you achieve this goal?"

I will share with you one other saying I like that I think holds people accountable.

"If I don't hear back from you, I will assume this job will be completed 100 percent. I don't need to go behind you and check on it, do I?"

Instilling a sense of ownership on the team takes a lot of the pressure off and any added pressure is the positive kind. It inspires them to contribute and to do good work. They own it! They are in charge. I trust them, and it is now their reputation that depends on the success of this job not only being completed but completed at a standard they are willing to put their name on!

What Will Be Your Legacy?

Did you ever think about what your personal and culinary legacy would be? I would guess that most of us don't. What I mean by legacy is, how does your last job, how will your current job and how will your next job all think of you and your ability to lead a team. How do they all think of you as a mentor, a disciplinarian or a leader? Will you be considered to be thoughtful, caring and genuinely interested in the future and personal growth of your staff? Will you be known for helping young people develop into great chefs? Will you be known as a chef of great integrity? I love that word integrity, because you can't fake integrity. Either you have it or you don't. Either you care about people or you don't. What will be your legacy? You have a choice to be great, you have the choice to make a difference in someone's life, what choice will you make?

Chapter 3

How Is Your Attitude?

This chapter is vitally important to your success as a chef leader, so it is imperative that you be honest with yourself. By now you have a feel for the direction of this book, my leadership philosophy, and how it can be applied toward building your ideal culinary team. The next chapters will introduce some helpful tools that will empower you to build a successful culinary program and get the most out of your staff.

Before we can get started, however, we need to determine your level of commitment. We need to find out what you are made of. You need to evaluate yourself and your professional values to establish a solid foundation toward becoming a respected leader. It always starts with you. Let's face it, you can hang all the signs on the walls you want and you can create mission statements, guiding principles, and policies, but the fact of the matter is that if you don't believe, if you don't lead by example, if you don't follow through, you might as well start a campfire with all the material you created, because your staff will not follow.

> **"What people say, what people do, and what they say they do are entirely different things."**
> —Margaret Mead, anthropologist

Passion Can't Be Faked

You can tell everybody how great your passion is, you can tell your boss how special it is, you can tell your fellow chefs how great it is, but they will *all* see through it if your own professional values are not as high as the ones you are preaching. You can't fake it! If you consider yourself a passionate chef, but you are not, it will not take people very long to figure it out. So either you believe or you don't—either you live it or you don't. It is up to you.

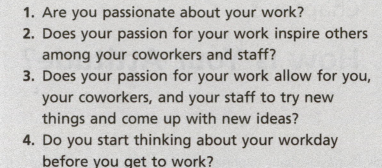

1. Are you passionate about your work?
2. Does your passion for your work inspire others among your coworkers and staff?
3. Does your passion for your work allow for you, your coworkers, and your staff to try new things and come up with new ideas?
4. Do you start thinking about your workday before you get to work?

If you answered *yes* to all of these questions, you are already a step ahead in establishing yourself as a great leader!

Identifying Values

The first step is to identify your professional values. The foundation for your professional life most likely includes the following:

Passion for Life
Culinary Passion
Passion to Build Great Teams
Commitment to Excellence
Determination
Follow-Through
An Honest, Caring Attention to Detail
Discipline
Dedication
Integrity

PASSION FOR LIFE

If you do not have passion for life it is difficult to have passion for anything else. My friend Dwight Edwards talks about passion for life in his book, *A Tale of Three Ships* (Charleston, SC: Booksurge LLC, 2005). Dwight lays out three basic courses of life a person can take—for some, though, life's greatest goal is survival. Read his book, you will enjoy it. Passion for life is where we all have to start.

CULINARY PASSION

Culinary passion is important and is hopefully the reason you are reading this book. It is easy to slide into a role of pumping out food and going home. Simply punching in and out is the way of life for many kitchens. It takes culinary passion to step out of this habit.

PASSION TO BUILD GREAT TEAMS

Now that you have the passion for great food, it is time to take care of the people who take care of you, the team that shares your passion. The what-have-you-done-for-me-lately routine no longer floats. One of the biggest secrets I can share with you here is that it feels good to help people, to make a difference in someone's life! Building great teams also means helping people to achieve their goals while they help you to achieve yours. "What comes around, goes around" is one of my favorite sayings.

COMMITMENT TO EXCELLENCE

This goes deep. Commitment to excellence means never, never, never sacrificing quality. NEVER! Most often quality takes longer, costs more, and is more difficult. It also takes research and requires never giving up until everyone agrees that the results are the best they possibly can be—at that moment. And the results can always be better the next time because we are older, smarter, and more experienced. On the golf course someone hits a drive into the woods—okay, usually me. But then I tee up my mulligan and hit a perfect ball—well, maybe not perfect but better. As my dad always says, "Same guy, just a little older."

> **"If you want to be successful, put your effort into controlling the sail, not the wind."**

DETERMINATION

As I said before, mean what you say and say what you mean. If you go around telling everybody you are going to write a book and then you don't, your word does not mean anything. "A man of integrity" may not be in the same sentence as your name. Be a strong person, have the determination to complete projects you say you will. If you tell everyone you are going to lose weight, do it! Make your word mean something. Don't give up because one of your goals is starting to become difficult or because it is no longer convenient.

FOLLOW-THROUGH

As you already know, follow-up is one of the most important qualities needed for all of the ideas in this book to work. Schedule, Empower, and Follow Up, or SEF, I discuss this concept in more detail in Chapter 4. Lacking follow-through is like having the most beautiful stove and no gas with which to cook. There is nothing more annoying than a weak follow-through. As a young person and a new professional, if you want to make a tremendous impression, if your boss asks something of you, follow through better than he could imagine. I can't tell you how many people don't have the where-withal to follow through on tasks. These are the employees who constantly get passed up for promotions. It is a simple idea that goes a long, long way.

> **"SEF: Schedule, Empower, and Follow Up!"**

AN HONEST, CARING ATTENTION TO DETAIL

Being plain honest is great. Having an honest, caring attention to detail is pretty special. The devil is in the details, as they say. If you don't pay attention to the details, it will show in the final results. When all of these values are broken down, you might think: What is the big deal?, they all make sense? What gets in the way of being a great person? Time, greed, heart, soul, caring?

INTEGRITY

What a special word is integrity. It is not a word you can throw around lightly. To know if someone has integrity it takes time to get to know them well and see them in action. If someone describes you as a person of great integrity, wouldn't you be proud? It is one of the greatest compliments a person can receive. To have great integrity is worth more than any culinary award you'll ever win. It is priceless.

The values you hold important in your professional life will be reflected in your work.

These are all outstanding qualities and foundation-setting values everyone should be proud of being associated with. You can add to this list every day, based on what is important to you and what you find motivational.

ASK YOURSELF THE HARD QUESTIONS

I recommend that before starting any of the programs and concepts I am going to share with you, you should sit down and spend some time evaluating your values. Ask yourself very tough questions about each value. Be honest in your answers, as this will only help you. For each value, give an example of the times you have performed well in relation to this value and also an example of a time your performance was not as stellar. I will dare to say we all can use some help in some areas. We are not going to be 100 percent in all categories all the time. It is very difficult to always perform at the highest level. So what are your weakest values? Is this an area where you always have problems or just some of the time? Identifying the problem areas will also aid you in determining how you can raise your performance level to be more successful.

Here is a short test for you to take. Score yourself from one to five, with five being the best.

I am cracking up as I write this, because I am on a plane sitting next to a businesswoman who is filling in one of these self-evaluation forms. I am thinking to myself, just give yourself all fives and be done with it. But, really, it is important to evaluate yourself as honestly as possible. If you can't trust yourself with your own answer, seems to me you are already failing.

Questions

1. Is your culinary passion true to your heart, or do you sometimes catch yourself telling your boss or your staff that you are going to do something but then don't?
2. Have you set goals for yourself and your team that were never accomplished? If so, does it happen often? Why aren't the goals achieved?
3. Do you walk your property and see things in other departments that are wrong but never make an attempt to correct them?
4. Have you ever put out a finished product that you knew in your heart was not up to your own standards?
5. When your boss asks something of you, do you complete the task better than he could have asked for?

You know how you scored on this quiz. If you gave yourself anything less than a five for each question, you have already identified areas where you can improve yourself. Now you know where to start!

Let me give you an example of how high standards can be compromised and indicate an area that needs to be improved: I saw a problem, but I did not follow through. The hospitality business goes 150 miles per hour, whether we are ready or not. If we have to feed 300 people at 8:00 P.M., there is only a certain amount of time we have to get the meal out. Many times I walk around the dining rooms and kitchens and see things that may be okay but not 100 percent. For example, I check on the dining-room lighting before a function. Around 4:00 P.M. in the afternoon, I would see that our buffet tables for that night were not properly lit. A thirty-foot ladder is needed to move the lighting, so this is no easy fix. I would make a mental note of it, and before the party started I realized that I had forgotten to have the lights changed. Even though it is not my job to fix the lighting, the lighting is part of the presentation of the meal, so it is important to have it done correctly. I saw the issue but dropped the ball by not having it corrected. I pride myself on my attention to detail, and I didn't *follow through* in this case. I have to be thorough; we all have to be thorough. If I see a problem and fail to resolve it before a member or customer experiences it, I have not done my job. Even though it was not my intention, the standards, the values I expect for the club were lowered because I did not resolve the problem. As managers, if we see a problem anywhere on the property, whether or not it is our department, we own the problem until it is resolved.

> To make sure that banquets run smoothly, I take all the BEOs (banquet-event orders) for a one-meal period, cut them to a size that fits in my breast pocket. During any one-meal period, I could have up to seven or eight BEOs in my pocket. As I walk through all the dining rooms and check station and buffet setups, I make note of any needs or changes on the corresponding menu. When I get back to my office, I double check all issues and resolve them—thus, the problems do not repeat themselves in future banquets.

It is up to you to set the standards you want for yourself and your department. No matter how busy we are, we have to be sure we keep our standard as high as possible. If a problem does manage to slip by unresolved to your satisfaction, hopefully your execution of other standards is so high that the end product is still great.

As I keep saying, it all starts with you. Are you happy with yourself, your job, and your kitchen? Because, if you are not, there is nothing I can say or do that will help you make your kitchen better. "It all starts at the top," as the saying goes. Your staff will often do what you do, even without prompting. In certain situations, they may act exactly as you act, simply because they are learning from you. So, if you are throwing pots around the kitchen, they will think it is an acceptable thing to do. Chances are you will work the way you feel. If you are not feeling well, you need to ask yourself why. By discovering the reasons behind the problem, you can turn it around to positive energy. I know when I start getting a bad attitude around the kitchen, it is usually because I am getting tired. You have to recognize this and do something about it!

Don't Carry Around Stress!

We all have a few things we enjoy doing for stress release. Hobbies or other nonwork-related activities provide "refueling" time. Exercising gives me great energy and a sense of release. I feel better about myself after doing it. I leave the house around 7:30 A.M. and work until around 2:00 P.M., then I try to go to the gym three days a week for a workout, return to the club around 4:00 P.M., and work until 9:00 or 10:00 P.M. Some of the employees or managers who don't really know my schedule will say, "he is always leaving," or "he is never here." I think it is a pretty honest schedule, as I am at the club during all three meal periods. I also do not leave if it is not possible. However, I can honestly tell you I am so much more productive in the first hour when I get back from working out, than if I stayed and worked for two hours. I have more energy, I am more focused, I am more productive, and I concentrate better on the projects I need to do when I get back. I find myself starting to crave these workouts, and the stress they relieve allows me to better focus on my work.

> "Do something about it! Stop complaining and do something about it!"
>
> —Torill Carroll

My wife Torill is now a fitness instructor. She inspires me to work out, mostly because she is so fit herself. I admire her strength and personal discipline. She will have coffee made, the kids' breakfast and school lunches made, a load of laundry going, and a thirty-minute workout completed before I get out of bed at 6:00 A.M.! Don't say you can't find the time after hearing that!

One morning before I made it a point to start working out, I was telling my wife how I felt fat and how tired I always was. A few days later I repeated the same story. After a few more days of bellyaching, she finally shouted to me: "Do something about it! Stop complaining, and do something about it!" Pretty much the story in life, wouldn't you agree? Nothing gets done by complaining. Only you can make it happen! Most importantly, people who feel good about themselves produce good results. It takes discipline to work out because you don't get results in just a day but gradually over time. You can't go to the gym and work out and lose five pounds in just a day. It takes time, and discipline is a wonderful character trait to have.

> **"Most importantly, think about this, people who feel good about themselves produce good results!"**

My point is that it is important for you to find something that works for you, whether it is working out or something else. Make the effort to relieve stress in your life. The more stress you carry with you, the less effective you will be at work and at home. It will help you focus your attention on what is important. I just love the feeling after a good workout. I hope I can inspire you here, because this kind of stress relief does the body and mind good.

> **"A little nonsense now and then is relished by the wisest men."**
>
> **—Willy Wonka**

Take a Vacation Already

You know when you are the busiest at your establishment and when things slow down. Early in the year or in advance, *schedule* your vacations. This was a mistake it took me a few years to figure out. Early on in my career, with all the traveling with the Culinary Olympic teams, culinary demonstrations, presentations, dinners, or whatever, I always told myself I would take a vacation when things slowed down or when there was an opening. The problem was, there is always something going on, always work to be done, always some commitment. As a result, I never took time off. Now, I schedule my vacation in advance: I plan on it, put it in the books, and look forward to it. We all need to see the light at the end of the tunnel, the reward for working hard. Look at it this way, there is ALWAYS going to be work on your desk! It is not going anywhere, and it will be right there when you get back.

We have talked about our own attitude, our kitchen atmosphere, and our professional values. Now let's take that knowledge and start building our program!

Chapter 4

Build Your Leadership Team First

Now that you have reflected upon what inspires you, thought about your ideal kitchen atmosphere, and identified the foundation of your professional values, you are ready to build your leadership team. The whole basis of my leadership team—and really the program as a whole—is what I call SEF: Schedule, Empower, and Follow Up. This will be discussed later in the chapter.

Build a Leadership Team

What is a leadership team? My leadership team is the team-within-my-team that helps me build my program. The first, and probably hardest, lesson every manager has to learn is that you can't do it all by yourself. The sooner you understand and accept that, the faster you will grow as a manager and the more effective you will be in putting together and directing your team. This team and the way in which you set it up will be your saving grace. That is why it is the first and most crucial step in building your program.

> **"The awesome thing about a team is that it can accomplish so much more than any one individual can, and at a higher quality level as well."**

There are three reasons for the leadership team—to (1) promote communication, (2) develop new programs, policies, and procedures, and (3) empower your employees to discuss any challenges to be met in building a better operation. The awesome thing about a team is that it can accomplish so much more than any individual can and at a higher quality level as well.

The leadership team should include the individuals that you determine have the most to offer your operation. They will be the individuals who display the most determination, heart, and soul and who possess the where-withal and desire to be great. All properties are different; but the beauty of this program is that it works for all size organizations. Whether yours is a kitchen of five employees or sixty, this program will work. Your leadership team may well consist of employees outside your department, and in fact that is actually encouraged. The more departments you get involved, the better chance the program has to be successful.

The Structure of the Leadership Meeting

At River Oaks Country Club, our leadership team consists of twelve individuals, from sous chefs and stewards to station chefs, all of whom have a great passion for our field, and even a tennis pro. Select your team on the basis of who you believe will excel in this environment and who will be of the greatest help to you. I also let the leadership team members know that they have been given the privilege to be a part of this team, but they have to earn the right to keep it.

When holding leadership meetings, don't hide the team away in a meeting room or even one of the dining rooms. I have a table in the kitchen for this meeting. Doing this will raise interest among the rest of your culinarians. They will wonder what it takes to be a part of this special team. Our meeting is held on payday every other week (everyone shows up for their check!). We have the meeting at 2:00 P.M., when business slows down a little.

Always have a printed agenda for the meeting. This keeps you organized and helps the meeting run smoothly. One of the best tips I can give you is to take minutes at these meetings. If minutes aren't taken, the meeting may just turn into a gripe session. Without minutes you lose control and account-ability. The reason for this goes back to the SEF concept—Schedule, Em-power, and Follow Up! Schedule the meeting, empower your employees to recognize challenges, put procedures in place to solve them, and follow up with them at the next meeting with the minutes.

> **"A good leader encourages followers to tell him what he needs to know, not what he wants to hear."**
>
> **—John C. Maxwell**

Assign leadership team members clear goals and objectives, give them deadlines, and make them follow up at the next meeting by holding them accountable to the group and for their assigned tasks. This is crucial to your success, the group's success, and the property's success. No one wants to come to a meeting only to be called upon when unprepared. To be unprepared in front of your peers is embarrassing. You have to follow up. If you don't, your staff will not take you or the meeting seriously. Then you have a real problem—apathy! Do you remember the feeling you had when you where a kid in school, the teacher asked the class for its homework and somebody (not me) was not prepared. Be firm at these meetings. Start out firm, and it will just become standard in your operation.

In addition to sending everyone a copy of the agenda before the meeting, I send out copies of the previous meeting's minutes the day after that meeting so everyone can follow along during the meeting, be reminded of their responsibilities, and be prepared to discuss what they have done to

The Leadership Team is a great way to include staff in the development process.

complete their tasks since the last meeting. Again, this is vital to proper follow up!

The key to your leadership team and the development of your program is to:

1. Schedule
2. Empower
3. Follow Up

It is no harder to remember than SEF!

This is a typical agenda for our meeting:

- Open with the culinary team's mission statement.
- Read the minutes from the last meeting.
- Review any assignments given out to the team.
- Present Sanitation Product Champion Report.
- Present Certification Product Champion Report.
- Present Stewarding Product Champion Report.
- Present Purchasing Product Champion Report.
- Assign new deadlines, if needed, on old items.
- "Go around the table." Let each chef give a two-to-five minute update on his or her department or station. Discuss any challenges. Open the discussion to resolve any issues.
- Hear executive chef's report on the property's schedule of events.
- Discuss sales and food cost.
- Assign new projects, goals, and deadlines.

I am willing to bet that 99 percent of all kitchens that have meetings don't keep minutes during their culinary meetings. How can any problems or tasks be followed-up on without minutes? Is anyone held accountable for anything? For example, one issue that was reported during one of our meetings was that the storeroom was continually being left unlocked. The team discussed how it was getting unlocked, reviewed our closing procedures, and documented the results. The leadership team was then responsible for relaying the policy to the rest of the staff.

In another example, the Sanitation Product Champion (I will discuss this concept later in the chapter) reported that the first in-house sanitation-inspection program started the previous week. The system seemed to work well; as a result, the team agreed we needed to add a column on the inspection form for maintenance issues. Because of the program, the chef in charge of inspection can report any maintenance issues, which are then transferred to a work order. One copy of the inspection form now goes to the club's general manager, one to the executive chef, and one to the head of maintenance. These are just a few examples of how the meeting proceeds. Ideas are talked about, fine-tuned, and then developed into policy, which the whole team is involved in. Important tip: If you are having problems getting things fixed at your property that pose possible safety hazards, you would be surprised how much faster they get fixed when the general manager gets a copy of what is reported week after week.

1. Organize
2. Focus
3. Assign tasks
4. Create deadlines
5. Follow Up!
6. SEF: Schedule it, empower your people, and follow up!

Another important practice and tool for these meetings is to give deadlines! Remember, everyone is busy, so you need to tell them what is expected of them and when. If assigning a task like developing a kitchen sanitation-inspection form, be sure to tell the team and the person responsible for creating the form when the first draft is due, record the due date in the minutes, and hold the team member accountable. If the task is not done by the due date, the person responsible will have to come to the next meeting and explain why it has not been done.

To aid the leadership team in staying organized and focused, each team member is given a three-ring binder in which all agendas and meeting minutes can be kept together. My leadership team is required to bring this binder to all meetings. It becomes their bible of policies, procedures, history, guiding principles, and mission statements. They will also use this binder for any meetings they may have with people in their department. I don't care if the line chef only has three other people on his team, I expect him to hold his own team meeting and require him to be organized and to set his own station goals. Let team leaders feel good about leading their team.

Leadership meetings are different from staff meetings. Leadership meetings are the core group, your coaching staff, the team that designs all the plays for the game and trains the players to be the best they can be. The leadership team *develops* the programs, policies, procedures; troubleshoots problems; and sets the standards for the team. Staff meetings consist of the entire culinary team, and these meetings are where you announce new programs and enforce them. I call our staff meetings Culinary Workout Sessions. They are held every six weeks with the entire culinary staff.

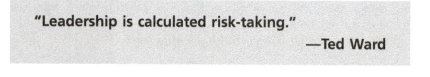

"Leadership is calculated risk-taking."

—Ted Ward

Now, the leadership team is considered to be a special group, as I discussed earlier. It is a privilege to sit at this table. Consequently, if a cook or chef comes to this meeting without fulfilling his or her assignment, the individual should have a good reason for it, or he or she will be asked to leave the table and come back when the assigned project is complete. Yes, the chef or cook is helping with a lot of work, but do not ever forget that the person is learning supervisory and program-building skills—this skill-building is a major component of the chef's or cook's professional development! This is very important: The purpose of the leadership team is not to decrease my workload. I am proud of the fact that I am teaching and growing my culinary team to be great leaders and team managers. There are very few properties teaching front-line cooks and sous chefs these skills. This program is "on-the-job training" for team management. This is a very special opportunity for any young person who is looking to grow into an executive chef position. This is why these people are willing to do the work; they see the value of learning and practicing new skills.

These resources and programs are priceless for them to learn in a live environment. I strongly believe this is why I have such a great crew with rare employee turnover. In fact, I have a file of applicants waiting to get into the program. I feel good about the fact that I am developing leaders within our team, a person others learn to respect as a leader. This is so important to me that it is part of our mission statement.

Product Champions

To further motivate and empower the staff, I implemented a Product Champions program. These are employees who champion a product and become the most educated and trained in that particular subject. For instance, we have a product champion at the property for the point-of-sales system. I like the title, because it has the word champion in it. Think about it. Doesn't everybody want to be a champion? Champions are great, they are winners, and they are the best of their kind. So, if I have a product champion of sanitation, this person is going to be the lead person on the program's development. I believe the title—product champion—shows confidence and trust, and it lends prestige to the concept. It also says, "Hey, I have a lot of responsibility." It also helps motivate the staff and recognizes the individuals who are doing a lot of work.

> **"The measure of success is not whether you have a tough problem to deal with but whether it is the same problem you had last year."**
> **—John Foster Dulles,**
> **former U.S. Secretary of State**

Typically, the more ideas, concepts, and programs I envision, the more frustrated I become. We all have some days where it takes everything we've got just to put out the business at hand. How is it possible to consider accomplishing so many programs? How many times have you thought of some great concepts, different menu styles, or staff incentive programs and just did not have the time to accomplish it? How do you find the time? That is the beauty of product champions. It makes so much sense, and your team is stronger for it, because they are part of the development process. Schedule, empower, and follow up (SEF). Empower your people to be a part of the process. Even when the departments are all running smoothly and efficiently, I can always see areas for improvement. Currently, there are four areas in our kitchen that I want to attack. New programs have to be written, new forms designed, and more communications implemented. There is no way I can do this all by myself, especially in the time frame that I want them completed...usually yesterday. So, I came up with four new product-champion areas:

PRODUCT CHAMPION OF SANITATION

This leadership team member is responsible for designing an inspection form (to be used in the club) based on the city's health inspection, report, and standards. This champion also puts together a team to ensure sanitation and safety standards are being met and schedules inspections of all the kitchens every week. There is no such thing as being too careful. This serves as a tool to provide a more sanitary and safe environment.

PRODUCT CHAMPION OF CERTIFICATION

My goal is to have more chefs in my kitchen certified by the American Culinary Federation (ACF) than any other club in the United States. This takes a little work and someone dedicated to help with the process. What better way to invest in your staff than to help them take the next step in their own careers, while at the same time making your kitchen stronger?

PRODUCT CHAMPION OF STEWARDING

I love this one! What department in your kitchen has the most turnover? In mine, it is stewarding. The leadership team member who heads this group is responsible for meeting with the group every four weeks. The stewarding team also meets at our kitchen table. The chefs serve appetizers, sandwiches,

Maintaining sanitation standards is vitally important for every kitchen.

and snacks to the stewards. We want them to feel special. We want them to know that we care about them and understand how important they are to our program. We give them an opportunity to talk about any challenges they currently have. You know what I was amazed to find out from one of these meetings? Many times the stewards work around a problem rather than report it. Sometimes they feel too intimidated to report a problem to the chef. So, instead of getting a piece of equipment fixed, they work around it.

We also go over their monthly review and discuss each steward's performance, which leads into the incentive program, which I will touch on later. The exciting thing about this area of discussion is that when you start talking about incentives and performance, the group loosens up a little. I was frustrated during the first few meetings and could not understand why the group would not open up. I think they were intimidated by the *Chef* sitting at the table. At the first meeting, nobody even ate an hors d'oeuvre. After the third meeting, when we awarded the incentives, they were eating and talking up a storm. I was so excited. They opened up, and we now get a lot accomplished.

PRODUCT CHAMPION OF PURCHASING

The leadership team member who heads this group researches better procedures for this department as well as works directly with our new computer-software programs and inventory-control systems. This product champion is also the liaison between the chefs and the purchasing agents. Other responsibilities include maintaining a current "burn-out" sheet for products that need to be moved (see Certificates and Forms).

These are just four examples of areas I wanted to improve on. And improvements have started to happen since product champions have been named. As a *team*, we have been able to accomplish so much in such a short time. To accomplish these particular programs would have taken me more than a year to complete on my own. What is more important here, however, is the *Empowerment* and *Follow-Through*. All my executive chef life I have been developing new programs here and there, as well as new policies and procedures, as all chefs do. But what is different here? What makes this system so much better?

1. You have a team helping you to develop programs, procedures, and policies.
2. You get a much more refined product with input from others.
3. The programs will be much stronger because of team involvement.
4. You will accomplish so much more in less time.
5. Your leadership team will be vested! They will believe. They will help monitor and maintain the programs so they will not fall apart.

6. Your leadership team members are learning valuable management skills.

> **"I not only use all the brains that I have, but all that I can borrow."**
>
> **—Woodrow Wilson**

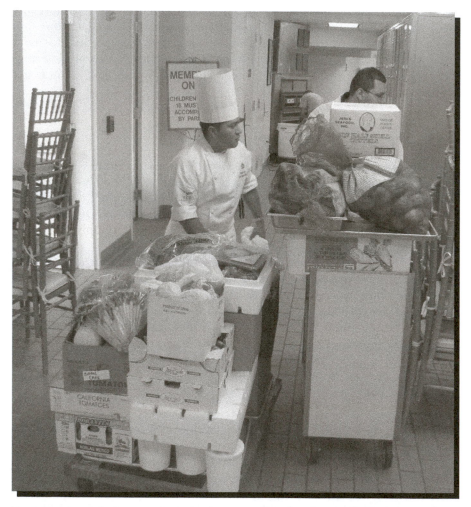

You can never do *too* much research or sourcing for that perfect product. There are too many great products available.

Input from Everyone

Many times I have come up with an original idea, floated it to the team, and had them come back with a concept ten times better. Look at it as a corporation or a club. How do you get things done efficiently and with expertise? Assign a committee chair, give them a goal, show them the direction in which you want to go, empower them to do it, and then follow up. This is so huge to me. First of all, we all win! Second, the other culinarians are learning how to build programs, and they are learning about team building and being part of a team. Third, they are vested in the program because they played a vital role in building the program. That is very important, so I am going to say it again. *They are vested in the program!* They believe because they helped develop it. How big is that? You can come up with programs all day long, but none of them will be worth the paper they are written on unless the team is on board and vested in the project. Again, SEF is vitally important, or you will fail. *Schedule* the meeting. *Empower* your employees to help design and research. *Follow Up* in the next meeting with the minutes and the assigned tasks.

> ## "They are vested in the program!"

So what areas in your current program need help, need improving, need more attention? New menu concepts, more contemporary station ideas for banquets, better pool menus, better cross training in your kitchen, or motivation, incentive programs, journeyman programs, employee dining? Whatever area you want to improve on, discuss it at your leadership meeting; collectively, the team will identify the problem, discuss ways of improvement, develop an action plan, make policy, and put it into action. This way you can have three or four major projects going at the same time and know that they all will be accomplished. Your product champions will develop their own team outside of the leadership meeting to attack the issue. Don't fall into the trap of thinking you can do it all yourself.

A New Kitchen Brigade

So what is the big deal? you may ask. This is nothing new, and I am sure you have heard all of this before. But how many kitchens have you heard of that are actually set up like this? In my experience, it has not been the chef's "nature" to set up his kitchen like a corporation. Why should it have been? The culinary kitchen brigade includes (and has for centuries) the garde-manger, saucier, *entremettier, poissonnier,* and so on. The chef set up the kitchen, ordered the food, instructed the staff, and the staff did exactly what the chef said—no questions asked. This is how we set up our kitchens. But, as I keep saying, the role of the chef has changed; therefore, the way in which we do things needs to change. Chefs are asked to meet with members and guests and to help plan, cost, style, and set up functions. Chefs are involved with directing front-of-the-house teams, and they have been promoted to general managers. Someone even made up a new culinary term "Chef & B," a play on the acronym F & B, that is, food and beverage. Some smaller operations have pushed responsibility for the foods and beverages onto the chef. This new era forces us to be thriftier with our time management, and this is what led me to devising these programs and writing this book.

So how are we successful? By scheduling, empowering, and following up, we are acting like CEOs. We need to build our organization and think of it as a corporation and set it up like a corporation. Then we will accomplish more together. Think beyond the traditional kitchen organization. If you intend to compete in this fast-moving business, you need to grow as an executive. It has worked for me, and my team has been able to get a boatload of work done because of it.

This concept came to me one day as I was leaving a department head meeting run by our club's general manager, Joe Bendy. I remember wishing I had all those managers working for me. I could get so much more work done! There would be twenty-five of us sitting in the room, and each of us had "homework" to do. Each one of us had to go back to our departments, develop, improve, excel, and report back the following week. If you were not ready for that meeting, you were called out.

> **"The only people who don't make mistakes are the people who don't do anything."**
> **—Phil Learned, CEC, AAC**

I had these same thoughts as I watched my good friend Chef John Folse run his meetings. I would think to myself, "If I had all those powerful people sitting around that managers' table like John, I could be that successful too." Well, guess what? I have a talented crew, too! And I bet you have a talented crew as well. This is how you are going to be successful. This is how your staff is going to grow and learn how to manage. This is how you are going to find time to be great!

No Excuses

> **"I won't live long enough to learn from my mistakes so I have to learn from the mistakes of others."**
>
> **—Joe Bendy**

The number of employees you have does not matter, whether ten, fifty, or hundreds. What is important is that you ask other key employees in the operation who you think may be great for their input, whether it is the dining-room manager, the assistant manager, or anyone else. I have our head tennis pro join our group, because he believes so strongly in team building. Come on, think outside the box.

How about the excuse that you can't get anybody to come to the meetings? Three thoughts come to mind from this. First, you are hiring the wrong people. It is vital to hire people who are motivated and who want to continue their professional growth. Second, if you lead, they will follow. Third, when you outline your goals at the beginning of the year, you can link it to performance bonuses. Talk to your general manager about it. It does not have to be a lot of money, just the idea that your staff is getting a bonus based on completing tangible goals. I have linked our certification product champion's success directly to his performance review and rewarded him for every team member he helps get certified.

> **"Great leaders are never satisfied with current levels of performance. They are relentlessly driven by possibilities and potential achievements."**
>
> **—Donna Harrison**

When I describe this concept to other people, they often ask how I get the leadership team members to do all this extra work. The answer is simple. This program is an incredible experience for them. They are learning how to build teams; build programs, policies, procedures, mission statements, guiding principles; develop organizational skills; and so much more. Think about how, traditionally, you did what the chef said and that was it. There was no debating of concepts. There was no team building.

Many properties don't necessarily help their sous chefs grow and train for first executive chef positions. It takes too long to get a really good sous chef and too long to train them, so why help push them out the door? I am blessed because our Green Beret program (see Chapter 12, "Green Beret Sous-Chef Program") is popular, and I have a line of great young chefs coming through the program. Our turnover rate is very low, and the team is young and hungry. It does not happen overnight, but it will happen when you offer this opportunity to your employees.

Communication

Let me say one thing about communication. When there is a breakdown, a problem occurs, or a mistake happens, most of the time you can track it to a communication breakdown. What a powerful statement! If that is the case, would it not make better sense to improve your own communication skills to cut down on what few mistakes you do make? It makes sense to me.

> **"Communicate, communicate, communicate—until you are sick of hearing yourself. Then communicate some more."**
> **—Jack Welch, former CEO of General Electric**

Think of a problem in your operation; track it back until you get to the root of the problem; and then see if I am not right. More often than not, someone did not tell somebody, did not explain clearly or it was not clearly understood, did not change a number, or forgot to copy something. As Phil Learned, CEC, AAC, of the Balsams Resort Hotel, once told me: "The only people who don't make mistakes are the people who don't do anything. It is OK to make a mistake, just don't serve it!" The secret is to learn from other people's mistakes.

Here is one example of a communication skill that works great for me. At the River Oaks Country Club, we average between sixty and seventy parties a week. The odds are against us making it through the week mistake-free. When I get a copy of the banquet events, I spend up to one-and-a-half hours going through the packet, making notes, plate drawing, and giving instruction to all departments. Then, on Friday, we make copies for all the departments, so everyone knows what is going to happen. Everything from the plate design to table layouts, even the recipe references are included. It is well worth my time to get it right at the beginning of the week rather than to scramble to get it right while handling the various other issues on the fly, sometimes explaining myself five times. Communication is the key. All sixty employees can read my thoughts rather than wait for me to speak to them personally. The less time I spend at the beginning of the week, the more time I have to spend explaining what I want in the following week.

I remember one time when I was scheduled out of town on business and our pool restaurant was switching from the summer to the post–Labor Day schedule. Some of our cooks were moved around because of school schedules, so we had two chefs that were not familiar with the menu for the station they were now working. As a precaution, I scheduled a senior chef to oversee the kitchen that night. I did not give any explanation why, I just scheduled it. That night the senior chef found himself with nothing to do. He went over the stations thoroughly with both cooks and left around seven o'clock. What I had failed to mention or to communicate to the chef is that I knew of a pop-up birthday party coming in at 7:30 P.M. for thirty people. On top of that, there was not a banquet-event order on the party because it was a late-notice event. Nor had banquet food been ordered, which was strike number two. Needless to say, the two chefs got hit all at once. The senior chef should not have left his scheduled shift, and I reminded him of that. But the bottom line was that I should have communicated better.

> **"There is nothing more annoying than a weak follow-through."**

Follow-Up

> When I got my first executive chef job, I wasted a lot of time handing out instructions one employee at a time instead of identifying the problem areas, developing the solution, and holding a meeting with the entire staff to make it policy. The employees will have absolutely NO follow-through if YOU don't have any follow-through. If you are too busy chasing your own tail, as I once was, you will find that you don't have time to run behind and check every employee's work. So we make policy as a team, we report our progress as a team, and everyone is held accountable that the policy stays in place.

As I have stated many times already, follow-up is one of the most important elements to your success while developing your programs. If you don't follow through, no one will take you seriously, and no one will attempt to finish the task you have assigned because you don't bother to follow up. There is nothing more annoying than someone who does not follow through. I judge the character of a person very highly when he or she has a follow-through rate of 100 percent. What a person! What a pro! I never have to go behind this person to see if he or she has done the job. With this particular character attribute, I know that he or she did the job and usually better than I expected. These people are very special. Remember that the next time your boss asks something of you. Not only do you drop everything you are doing to get his request done, you go above and beyond his expectations. This is a very simple formula. What kind of employees do you want working for you? When you get that one employee who not only finishes an

Making notes on event orders clarifies plans for all chefs involved.

assigned task but also goes above and beyond, that is the employee you will come to trust and who will earn a promotion. That is also the employee you have to be. There is nothing more annoying than a weak follow-through!

The reason behind this discussion is to stress that the leadership team will do whatever you tell them. The secret is that *you must tell them.* Communicate! They have to understand. You cannot change on the fly and be successful. You cannot be successful if you are instructing only one person at a time. At one of the first executive chef jobs I had, I would walk from one end of the kitchen to the other and see ten things that needed to be changed or addressed with the staff. At first, I would stop and point out to each employee how to do the procedure differently. Two days later, I would have to stop and tell a different employee the same thing. What is the lesson? Take notes, develop your new operating policies, and present them to your entire team during your "culinary workout sessions," or staff meetings. Once that is done, everyone should be on the same page.

1. Identify the problem.
2. Develop the solution.
3. Make a policy.
4. Educate the entire staff at the same time of the new policy.
5. Follow through.

Now that we have the leadership team together, your first goal is the Mission Statement.

Chapter 5

What Is Your Mission?

What Is a Mission Statement?

Amission statement declares your company's goals, summarizing what you are trying to accomplish. An effective mission statement should tell your company's story in less than forty words. What makes having a culinary mission statement exciting is the way in which it forces us to think about what are our team's goals, other than excellent food. It is not just about the food. The mission is what *you* and *your team* stand for and why you do it. Some people may read this and say: "That sounds good, but I don't have time to go through all that. I'm going to skip this part. I don't need a mission statement." You can skip it, but it will be difficult for you to accomplish anything else described in this book if you don't have a mission statement! It will be difficult for you to create a true team if you don't allow your staff to be a part of developing the mission. When you do this and see the difference it makes with your employees, when they can be a part of something special, it reinforces—yet again—that they are vested employees. This is one of the very first steps in your culinary team's development, don't skip it. It establishes the foundation for everything to come.

Why Create a Mission Statement?

Why is a mission statement important? If the property has a mission statement, why does the kitchen need one? Do you have goals? I hope that you do. What is the purpose of the goals? What are they meant for you to accomplish? If you don't have goals, you are just punching in and out, working aimlessly day after day. You should have long- and short-term goals, both personally and professionally.

> **"If you don't have goals, you are just punching in and out, working aimlessly day after day."**

I am required to present my goals every year to the club's general manager, and he bases my performance review on it. A very dear mentor and friend, Dr. Noel Cullen, CMC, once told me, "Once you put something on paper, you own it." Once I put those goals on paper and submit them to my boss, you better believe I own them. Now I have to achieve them. Part of my paycheck rests on achieving those goals.

How can you achieve your goals, or the goals of the property, if you don't have them written down? How can you shoot a bull's-eye if there is no target? It would be like trying to hit a home run with a large blanket hanging in front of the batter's box, blocking the pitcher. How can you hit the ball if you can't see the pitcher! You get the idea.

> **"You need a mission for your staff, an overall objective, and a clear sense of where your team is going."**

The same goes for your staff. Every organization has a mission statement, a purpose, and a reason for being. If you currently have a mission statement for your team, when was the last time you reviewed it, much less updated it? This is important. A mission statement is meant to be a living document. Are your goals the same now as they were twenty years ago, or even two years ago? You should constantly review the mission statement with your staff and constantly fine-tune it.

What Goes into a Mission Statement?

You need a mission for your staff, an overall objective, and a clear sense of where your team is going. The goals and mission for the culinary team are much different than those of the golf department. One of my favorite books is *High Five* (New York: HarperCollins, 2001). This is a fun book that talks about building great teams and getting the most out of your players. It is a quick read and a charming story. One of its most powerful messages is that "none of us are as smart as all of us" (pages 60, 93, and 144). You have probably heard about or read the *One Minute Manager* (New York: Berkley Books, 1983), written by Kenneth H. Blanchard and Spencer Johnson. This book is a timeless piece that really makes you think about how you run your team. How do you spend your time during your day? What is your management style? It teaches how to get more out of your staff and how to set goals. From reading these books, I understand now why managers have a whole team helping them. Anyway, these books are fun reads, inspirational, and practical. If you have not read either of them, I highly recommend you do so.

In *High Five,* Blanchard et al. outline their ideas about how to provide clear purposes and values, as follows:

- "Create a challenge, a reason for being, a "Holy Grail" that commits and motivates people to work together."
- "Set clear and compelling goals and strategies, for the individual and the team."
- "Be clear on your values."
- "Create a team charter that formalizes commitments to each other and clearly states what the team wants to accomplish, why it is important, and how the team will work together to achieve results."*

Creating Your Mission Statement

As you create your mission statement, consider that your team's answers to the following questions should be answered in the final statement.

1. What is the purpose of your culinary team?
2. What are you currently doing to address the needs of your culinary team?
3. What principles, belief, or values currently guide your culinary team?

One thing is for sure, you cannot copy anyone else's complete mission statement. You can, however, gather information and inspiration from many other mission statements. But only your team can develop *your* mission statement.

I have given hundreds of tours of our new facility and handed out just as many orientation packets, mission statements, and guiding principles. I tell each recipient that I am very proud to share all of the hard work of the team and that I hope that they can use it as a guide in their own careers at the club and in developing their own programs.

You cannot force your personal culinary guiding principles down the throats of your employees. Your leadership team has to collectively develop its own guiding principles, goals, and mission statement, and they must fit with the mission statement of the whole organization and, specifically, your culinary program. Wait until you start having conversations with your lead-

---

* *Source:* Ken Blanchard, Sheldon Bowles, Don Carew, and Eunice Parisi-Carew, *High Five* (New York: HarperCollins Publishers Inc., 2001), p. 189.

ership team about these concepts. You will be surprised at how energized they get. Chances are they have never been asked to take part in the development of such concepts. This is just another way in which they will gain a vested interest in the program!

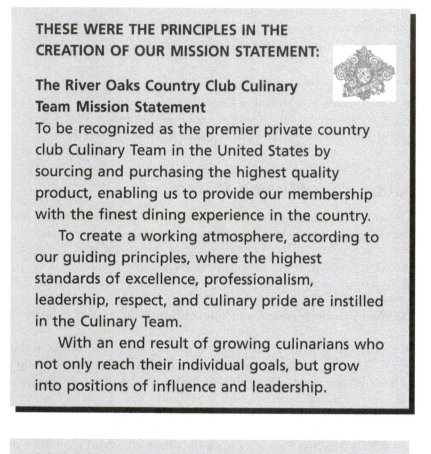

THESE WERE THE PRINCIPLES IN THE CREATION OF OUR MISSION STATEMENT:

The River Oaks Country Club Culinary Team Mission Statement

To be recognized as the premier private country club Culinary Team in the United States by sourcing and purchasing the highest quality product, enabling us to provide our membership with the finest dining experience in the country.

To create a working atmosphere, according to our guiding principles, where the highest standards of excellence, professionalism, leadership, respect, and culinary pride are instilled in the Culinary Team.

With an end result of growing culinarians who not only reach their individual goals, but grow into positions of influence and leadership.

"Your leadership team has to develop guiding principles, goals, and mission statements that fit your organization and your program."

I cannot emphasize these points strongly enough. If you have never sat around a table and genuinely listened to your staff—the leaders of your kitchen—and listened to what is really important to them, specifically, it may be difficult to understand fully what I am saying. When your team has an opportunity to let its guard down and speak freely about what it believes is important; it is not until then that you will see new excitement in the eye of your team. When you can have an open discussion on the development of a mission statement with your team and they are part of that, it becomes special. When the statement is made into a sign and posted in your kitchen for the first time, you will see the pride in your team's eyes. When you hear your staff talking about it, explaining the mission to others, you will feel a sense of pride you have not felt in a long time.

Read the Mission Statement, Often!

> **"They will grow into positions of influence and leadership."**

Our mission statement is read during every leadership team meeting, every employee review, and once a week during the one-a-day meetings. It is important that all employees understand the mission statement, believe in it, and have a chance to comment on it. When I am in my office and I hear the mission statement read by a team member at the beginning of our one-a-day meetings, I am so proud. We read it every week. Recently, one of my hard-working, Mexican garde-manger chefs read it for the first time at the meeting. Her English was very good, but she was nervous. Six months ago, I don't think she would have even tried to read it; but on that day, all the employees gave her an ovation when she was done reading the statement. It was awesome! I can't speak Spanish, let alone read it. She did fantastic, and everyone felt great about it.

I really love our mission statement. Obviously, we want to serve the best food possible. Being a country club, we have the luxury of buying only the best products we can find, mostly because the members expect it, and they pay dearly to be members. The second part of the mission is something I am extremely proud of: Creating the best culinary kitchen atmosphere possible and helping our culinarians take the next step in their careers. I have had many chefs move on to their first executive chef positions with great benefits and salary *because* they were part of the team here and were encouraged to grow and learn.

Setting Goals

There are currently ten of our chefs competing in culinary competitions, including the United States Culinary Olympic Team and Chaîn des Rôtisseurs and local competitions. It is a very young, talented, and hungry kitchen.

Reading the culinary mission statement every week serves to remind all employees of the goals of the whole team.

Competitions are not everything, and you do not have to compete to be successful, but they do open doors for you. They provide many opportunities, allow for world travel, and challenge chefs to study and work harder than ever before. You meet chefs you never would have met had you not been involved. It is true that competitions are not for everyone, but the people who choose to compete and stay with it benefit tremendously. The reason I am spending so much time on this is that those who compete in my kitchen succeed and have a special drive. They have goals and are self-motivated. They will grow into positions of influence and leadership. Now it is my job to find out what I can do to motivate the rest of the staff, to find out what are each and every one of my employees' goals so that I can help them to realize them.

For example, one of my cooks loves to carve ice, so I introduced him to a local ice carver, and he now works for him part time. Other chefs have been interested in working at resorts, so I hooked them up with a two-month experience at a resort that was busy during our slow time. Make sure you teach all of your staff and not just the shining stars.

Not all of your staff is going to be so motivated, not all of your staff will want to compete, not all will even set personal goals for themselves. This is why it is important that you recognize the different levels of talent and ambition within your staff. The more you understand your staff, the better chance you will be able to help them excel. Not all of them will even want to excel. I'm sure there are employees here and there who just want to punch in and punch out, get paycheck, and go home. I have made it a rule that we are only going to hire culinarians, and I try to be as clear as possible during the interview process that this *is not* a punch-in, punch-out job. They are told coming in that they will be pushed often to excel and that they are expected to climb the ladder of success and strive to improve professionally.

A good skill you can practice here is to identify your staffs' individual goals during their individual sit-downs or reviews. During this one-on-one, you have an opportunity to understand more about your employee and to find out what is important to them. In some cases, you may have to dig. In some cases, what is really important to the individual may not be cooking or the job at all, it may be just trying to survive with the challenges at home. Obviously, our expertise is culinary and not psychologic, but sometimes just listening is good. Sometimes simple, kind gestures (and the fact that you care) helps a lot. We do what we can when we can. Most importantly, ask the individual what they want to achieve over the coming year. Ask them specifically what skills they would like to practice or acquire. Don't end the meeting until you can agree on something the two of you can accomplish together. Write these goals into the review and refer back to it every four months. Place a date in your calendar for follow-through. Schedule it, and follow up! You will feel pretty good when you have made a difference in someone's life!

One of our latest Product Champion projects was to review and revamp our annual employee review form so that it fit our guiding principles better and allowed room for the employee and the chef to recognize and record the employee's goals for the upcoming year. Chances are your property has a yearly review for all employees that is a rubber-stamped form for the entire property. I thought that our culinary team would be better served during the review period, if we could customize our review to fit what is really important to our skill in the kitchen. More importantly forcing the employee to think about personal and professional goals that we can work on together. These should be measurable goals that the chef and employee can review every year. I believe this is going to be a great tool for us in the future.

> **"A successful man is one who can lay a firm foundation with the bricks others have thrown at him."**
>
> **—David Brinkley, television journalist**

The goals set for a person complement the department's mission statement as well as foster that employee's professional growth. In turn, the department's overall goals and mission statement complement the club's mission statement. It is one healthy circle. You can't build a house without a foundation. You can't put the roof on without a frame. You can't stamp a goal on your culinary team without reaching deeper into your staff. Start building your foundation, and the rest of your house will be strong.

Chapter 6

The Principles That Guide Us

Now that your mission statement is written, you can challenge your leadership team to develop its Guiding Principles. The guiding principles are the backbone of your operation. They should be the ideas, values, and beliefs that guide your work and your culinary team's work on a daily basis. That is why it is so important to take time out of your busy schedule to develop them with your team. This is yet another way they will be vested in their work!

While you were developing your mission statement, your leadership team hopefully came to the table with all kinds of ideas that they considered important enough to be part of the mission statement. Be sure they save all of their idea notes from the mission statement–development sessions whether they were used or not. After all, everything you work on as a team is priceless information for use when you might need to start your own team and build your own values as an executive chef. The leadership team meetings will be the most valuable education an individual will ever receive, because they are real and show how to apply the situations to your own program development. Members are a part of something special, which is hard to find. How to build great teams? This kind of experience cannot be bought, and you need to be sure leadership team members understand how special it is to be a part of such a program. I know I've touched on this several times already, but it just can't be said enough.

> **"You've got to love your people more than your position."**
>
> —John C. Maxwell

RIVER OAKS COUNTRY CLUB CULINARY GUIDING PRINCIPLES

As a proud member of the River Oaks Country Club Culinary Team, I am committed to:

1. Improve everything we touch.
2. Taste everything.
3. We are ladies and gentlemen serving ladies and gentlemen.
4. Commit to excellence.
5. Treat our members and each other with respect and dignity.
6. Create a positive and safe work environment.
7. Use the proper tool for the proper job.
8. Be accountable.
9. Serve hot food hot and cold food cold; never serve an inferior product.
10. Uncompromising levels of sanitation and cleanliness.
11. Take pride in the chef uniform; be clean and crisp.
12. Prepare ultimate kitchen and mental "mise-en-place."
13. Never lose a member.
14. Meticulously attend to every detail.
15. Be an ambassador of the ROCC Culinary Team.
16. Recognize and reward excellence.
17. Educate and motivate.
18. Consider "What are our options?"
19. Always ask, "What can I do to help?"
20. Function as a team.

So, when it comes time to develop the guiding principles, work with everyone's mission statement notes. The ideas that perhaps didn't make it into the mission statement are still valuable. Chances are many of these ideas and values will end up in the team's guiding principles.

This process took our leadership team over three months to develop. It was pretty exciting to see all the chefs involved with the process and to hear their points of view. We constantly refined the guiding principles until everyone was satisfied. To this day, we continue to refine both the guiding principles and the mission statement. I believe strongly that you have to continue to evaluate how you operate and how you do business, which changes every year.

Now when I said it took our team over three months to develop our guiding principles, do not get discouraged. We were also working on the orientation packet and product champions program at the same time, which I would not recommend. Also, when I tell you it was fun, I truly mean it. It was a blast. I think I speak for the entire team when I say we were excited to meet at the table every week. Again, I started this whole concept in the month of August, which is our slowest time, and at the time, we met every week because I wanted to accelerate the process. As outlined before, there was a lot of other business to be done at the leadership meetings and the development of the guiding principles was only part of it. That is why it took us so long.

So we had everyone's input, shuffled it, wrote it down, continued to highlight the ideas that were most important to us, refined some more, until we came up with a final twenty principles. Many of the guiding principles were long, so we had to narrow them down and make them more precise. I felt that if we had more than twenty principles, people would forget them, and so we focused on our top twenty.

Guiding Principle of the Week

After a year of working on this program, we decided to have a guiding principle of the week. We started out with a principle of the day, but we felt we could better drive the principle home if we talked about it for a whole week. Each leadership team member is responsible for going over the principle of the week during their one-a-day meeting, which I will explain in Chapter 7. Behind each of the guiding principles, we have bulleted back-up material to support them. Below are a few examples.

TO IMPROVE EVERYTHING WE TOUCH

- Constantly look for ways to improve the taste and quality of the food.
- Develop better ways of presenting and serving food.
- Improve the operations of the kitchens.

- Continually find new ways to bring all aspects of the culinary department to a higher level.

TASTE EVERYTHING

- Use disposable tasting spoons.
- Evaluate the flavor of the food during each level of preparation.
- Taste the final product before it is served.
- Rate the flavor quality of all raw products (i.e., nuts, fruits, vegetables, etc.).

WE ARE LADIES AND GENTLEMEN SERVING LADIES AND GENTLEMEN

- Maintain the highest level of professionalism.
- Be courteous.
- Treat others as you would have them treat you.
- Speak in a respectful tone.
- Politeness and manners are key.

COMMITMENT TO EXCELLENCE

- Every team member must participate in improvements.
- Live the guiding principle each day.
- Stay motivated and positive and keep things moving in a positive direction.
- Believe in the team and its potential.
- Dedicate yourself to always do your best.

Copies of the guiding principles and the back-up material are in the Leadership Manual, which all leadership team members have and which they can refer to during the meetings. I also have pocket-sized, laminated cards printed in Spanish and English for each member of the culinary team to carry on their person at all times. This is great because if ever there is an issue, we can ask the employee to pull their card out so that we can discuss the problem. Also, these cards serve as yet another form of reinforcement of our program, another reason our program will not fall between the cracks. We also post the guiding principle of the week in all kitchens so all chefs can refer to it.

It is not enough just to come up with a good idea, you have to live it! Empower your teams to ensure that your program survives.

Chapter 7

Program Survival: Living It!

Now that we have spent all this time researching, meeting, developing, and producing these great programs, what do we do to be sure they don't fall through the cracks and fail? How many times have you been to a convention or a seminar, listened to great operational ideas or motivational speakers, returned to your property, pumped your staff up about everything you heard, put some policies in place, and then two weeks later, it is as if nothing ever changed? It happens all the time. I have decided that this is not going to happen to my programs ever again. We put far too much work into them to let them fall by the wayside, and besides, my crews are all vested! Here are some of the ways we have been able to keep all our programs going strong.

> **"He who has done his best for his own time has lived for all times."**
> **—Friedrich von Schiller, playwright**

Keep the Program Strong

LEADERSHIP TEAM

I need to mention the leadership team again, as they are the soul, the heartbeat of everything. If your leadership team is not on board, nothing will survive. After all, it is virtually impossible for the leadership team not to be vested in the program, because they created everything. The point I need to drive home here is how important it is to schedule your meetings religiously—the same time, the same day of the week—so everyone counts on it. These meetings need to become part of your operational procedures. Schedule it, empower your team, and follow up.

ONE-A-DAY MEETINGS

One-a-Day, like the vitamin, that is how I look at it. The information shared in these meetings should be essential for the day. In your operation, big or small, you have people who make salads, desserts, sauté, poach, and broil. Most operations either have à la carte dining, banquets, or both. Other operations, like mine, have a bakeshop, butcher shop, garde-manger, and so on. Regardless of the size of your operation, I would recommend each department have a one-a-day meeting. The person in charge of the department should run the meeting, and you should be at as many meetings as you can for support and validation.

During this meeting, the leadership team member goes over the day's events and responsibilities and reviews the guiding principle of the week. Review any new policies and discuss any recent challenges and ways to improve the operation. The staff is encouraged to interact. This is how and when we reinforce our mission statement and guiding principles.

I recommend the one-a-day meetings only take five-to-seven minutes. We hold ours in the kitchen at the stations. This is when the leadership team member will bring out the binder of all back-up material for all programs as well as the guiding principles, current kitchen policies, procedures, kitchen programs, and personal notes. It is important the leadership team member reviews all the information he or she received in the Leadership Team meeting with the line employees. We discuss what parties we have that day, assign responsibilities, discuss china, and confirm the menus. This is a great tool, which many of you probably already use in some fashion or another. Just be sure you are taking full advantage of the team being together. This is a great opportunity to discuss teamwork and to support the mission and guiding principles.

GUIDING PRINCIPLE CARD

All our employees are required to carry their guiding principles card on their person while at work. The card is a reminder of our beliefs, and it helps solidify how important is this program.

KITCHEN SIGNAGE

Now I am not talking about handwritten signs. We design and print our signs, using Microsoft Publisher, and laminate them. I spend some time with the design and layout. I post our mission statement, our guiding principles, and

One-a-day meetings help keep everyone involved focused on the day's work ahead.

any motivational sayings on the kitchen walls. I also make sure the club's logo is on everything.

It is important that you start establishing your brand at your property. All our signs, notices, schedules, and recipes have our logo on them. I tell the employees—if it has our logo on it, we are guaranteeing that it is going to be great. This helps drive home our mission. It becomes part of our working environment.

> **"Success is never final, failure is never fatal, it is courage that counts."**
>
> **—Winston Churchill**

CULINARY CERTIFICATE FOR NEW EMPLOYEES

It is important that all new employees who enter the River Oaks Country Club (ROCC) Culinary Program understand that they are a brand new member of a very special team. The need to feel proud and special from day one. We print professional certificates complete with a gold ROCC Culinary Team seal and a red ribbon. This is a framable document they can be proud of. Again, this is yet another sign of my commitment to the employee and his or her importance to the operation.

CULINARY WORKOUT SESSIONS

As I mentioned before, workout sessions are the *complete culinary team meetings* held every six weeks. This is the meeting when I address every single employee in the department. This is when the executive chef gives the "state of the union address." We accomplish a lot of work during a short amount of time. The meetings usually last less than an hour and are held in a banquet room with soft drinks available. The workout sessions are designed to be a time when all employees can voice their opinions, sound their challenges, and suggest new ideas and concepts to help improve everyone's workday. To help stimulate conversation, leadership team members record some of the challenges during the one-a-day meetings so they can touch on them with the whole team.

New employees are introduced and presented with their ROCC team certificate. At some meetings we will have a guest speaker or the general manager will address the staff. We go over any new policies or procedures, and then we recognize and reward excellence and hand out gold cards for those who have been nominated by their peers (this and other incentive programs are discussed in Chapter 11).

These sessions have become a very special time, as we need to praise our staff as often as possible. Many work environments do not take enough time to give well-earned praise publicly. Often our schedule is so busy we take our employees for granted. Publicly recognizing employees for their excellent work reinforces the team environment and demonstrates, yet again, that they are vested. They are LIVING IT!

MANAGERS' MEETING

Don't forget your weekly managers' meeting. In just about all properties today, there is a managers' meeting, department heads' meeting, or executives' meeting. Whatever your property calls it, remember that it is (or can be) a big part of your culinary team's success. Again, it is all about communication. The staff and the property need to know what kind of programs you are building in your department. This helps in many ways, including the following:

1. Your team will be an inspiration to the rest of the group.
2. You will be looked upon as a leader, not only of the culinary team but an important leader of the property for being proactive in your management approach.
3. You will find that success and positive energy will start rubbing off and onto your colleagues.
4. The front of the house will start bragging about all of your programs to the guests, members, and public.
5. When you start sharing all of your hard work, you will find people in other departments will increase their respect for you, your team, and everything you do.

If there is any chance for communication, we need to take advantage of it. What better way than to share these programs with the management of the property.

PROPERTY NEWSLETTERS AND WEB SITES

Communication! Is it starting to ring in your head? Yes, communication is key, and what better way to communicate to your audience than through the company's newsletter or Web site. If you are not doing this already, be sure you begin to contribute an article to every relevant newsletter. Share with your customers all of the special things you are doing to be sure they enjoy their culinary experience. When customers learn about all of your team's success, it will renew their interest in your operation, and they will have added comfort in knowing that they are dining at a professional establishment. You will not believe how proud your staff members will be to see their names in print or pictures of them receiving gold cards; it all helps build culinary pride.

All properties today have Web sites. If you don't have a presence on the site already, make a case to your general manager that you would like to be on the Web site to promote your team and everything you are currently doing to ensure your customers a fabulous culinary experience every time they dine at the property.

INCENTIVE PROGRAMS

These programs are discussed in Chapter 12 more fully, but it is important to mention them here. What keeps your programs going strong is a strong staff. A strong staff comes from great leadership. Great leadership constantly acknowledges, recognizes, and rewards its staff. This is vitally important. Sometimes we get so wired into the project at hand, we forget to acknowledge the ones who help us to succeed. This happened to me. I was so excited about our leadership team's progress, I forgot to stop and thank them. After about a year and a half, one of my team members approached me and said, "Chef, don't you think it would be a good idea to have a little leadership party to reward everyone on a job well done. It has been over a year, and the team has been working full steam since we started." I could not believe I overlooked this. While I try and have a cookout party for the entire staff every year, I needed to do something formally for the leadership team, which is the heartbeat of the operation. The cliché of "what have you done for me lately" does not float with great leadership teams.

GOAL SETTING AND REVIEWS

As we talked about before, helping your staff realize their goals can be a wonderful employee-enrichment exercise. A great time to do this is during their review or at individual sit-downs. One great incentive that I am proud of is having our club sponsor anyone wishing to gain certification by the American Culinary Federation (ACF). This can be a little pricey, but it is a great benefit for the employees. So important is this to me that we developed the Certification Product Champion to help assist these individuals to accomplish their goals.

> **"You only get out of it, what you put into it!"**
> **—Joe Bendy**

Communicate Success

No smoke and mirrors here, it is all about *communication*. Driving your mission statement home and putting checkpoints in your operation encourages your staff to continue to communicate the guiding principles. SEF: Schedule, Empower, and Follow Up. You have the choice, either *Find time to be great* or don't. When you add value, you find value! You can be a punch-in and punch-out employee for a while, until you are found out, or you can strive to be great—schedule your time to be great! It is your choice. If you decide on the easy road, don't ever complain about how much you get paid or how little you enjoy your career. Always remember, *what comes around goes around.*

Chapter 8

Educational Environment

O ne of the best ways to get quality people to work for you is to create a genuinely educational environment. What do you have to offer as an executive chef? What is the atmosphere in your kitchen? This is really the main factor to consider. Is the atmosphere fun, educational, productive, challenging, friendly, precise, and professional? There is only one executive chef in charge in your kitchen, and it is up to him or her to set the tone for the kitchen. Chances are that many of the other cooks in your kitchen also aspire to be chefs and someday executive chefs. It is my experience that the one thing quality employees desire most is *education.*

Encouraging an educational environment will prove to be the most valuable asset in your operation, I promise. It is about how you can make a difference in the lives of your staff. What a powerful thing, making a difference in someone's life. How can you do this? *Schedule it!* It will not happen unless you make it happen. Yes, you are busy; but if you schedule it and make the time for it, the rewards will be visible immediately. Put a calendar on your desk and schedule time for your employees.

Have you ever noticed that young children often absorb whatever environment they are in? Let me give you an example: My wife is Norwegian, and she speaks Norwegian to the kids and has since they were babies. As soon as they started speaking, they knew that they had to speak one way to Papa and another way to Mama. They sorted out the English language from the Norwegian language, and they address us respectively. That is amazing to me. Fifteen years later, I still do not understand what they are saying. Young and new professionals are the same way. They are eager to learn and (usually) adapt well to their environment. My point is that you should surround your employees with a consistently great educational environment; in turn, your staff will absorb what you teach them.

> "Genius? Nothing! Sticking to it is the genius! I've failed my way to success."
>
> —Thomas Edison, inventor

Teach Something New Every Day

Here are nine educational offerings and opportunities I've put into place for my staff:

CULINARY DEMOS

Present a culinary demonstration for your staff several times a year. Your staff is hungry for education. They will enjoy whatever you have to offer. This is also a good time to allow anyone in your culinary team to give a fifteen-to-twenty-minute presentation. Because I am in Texas, I have a wide range of talented chefs who specialize in Tex-Mex, Mexican, and barbecued foods, to name the obvious ones. I am sure almost every cook you have has a favorite recipe he or she does well. The culinary demos give your staff an opportunity to stand in front of their peers and share their skills, expertise, and recipes. Public presentations are not a skill everyone has; they may be uncomfortable in such a position; and these demonstrations provide a great opportunity to practice and grow more comfortable. It is also an opportunity to learn a lot about each other. One time I started a signature sandwich competition; the winning entrant received a $100 prize and the sandwich was included on the lunch menu. This is really kind of fun; everyone is already pretty competitive, so it presents a healthy environment. We treated it very seriously, with blind judging by the club's president, general manager, and a maître d'. The winner also got their picture in the club's newsletter. It was a very motivating challenge on many levels.

LEADERSHIP MEETINGS

For my leadership team meetings, I have twelve salaries sitting around the table for one hour, as everyone is away from their designated tasks, so it is important to me that we are not meeting for the sake of meeting. We have to accomplish something for the betterment of the team. That is where the reading and taking of the minutes come in handy; the minutes help to keep everyone focused on the goals. As you know by now, the leadership team is the heartbeat of the system, so why not introduce some education at these meetings. In this case, the leadership team is an education in itself, but I like to push a little more. River Oaks Country Club (ROCC) is so blessed to have a motivational speaker on staff. His name is Dwight Edwards, and he is a published author who speaks all over the country. He also happens to be a tennis pro and someone who works well with kids. I have asked him to join our leadership meetings, and he gives a five-to-seven-minute lecture that is incredibly motivating. Look around your property; I am willing to bet you have talented people all around you who are willing to share a lesson with your staff. It is amazing to hear about other managers or employees' hobbies or stories. We all can learn from each other. Hearing the stories of others can spark conversation, and usually the stories include some lessons to be learned. This creates a great culture of respect.

> **"No man will make a great leader who wants to do it all himself or get all the credit for doing it."**
> **—Andrew Carnegie, industrialist**

ONE-A-DAY INFORMATIONAL MEETINGS

Each department in your kitchen should have one-a-day meetings. These work on the same premise here as the leadership team meeting. A great tool that we use in these meetings is to talk about what went right and what went wrong prior to the meeting. To reflect on the day while it is fresh in everyone's mind guarantees a better result. This is educational. It is also just a few minutes long.

DISTINGUISHED VISITING CHEFS PROGRAM

Invite local chefs to give one-hour demos for your team *or* prepare a special chef's dinner for a visiting chef. I have a lot of fun with this program. Make it a permanent program! Develop the guidelines with your leadership team.

Why do you need to develop a program? I try to think of it as a university. Remember all those "ask-yourself questions" exercises (in Chapter 1) we talked about? Well, here we go again. I asked myself—if I had to build the best visiting chef program, how would I go about it? what would be my model? and how could I make it better? Think big!

When thinking about a visiting chef program, consider who does it the best and what can you do to make it better? Now, all of a sudden, the visiting chef series we developed is prestigious. Chefs' pictures are included on our Wall of Fame. We give framed certificates to the visiting chefs and signed bottles of wine and gifts. We also open it up to our club members. The team identifies talented chefs in the Houston area that they would like to meet. A schedule is devised and printed, and now we have a program. Include your leadership team on all programs. You will have fun developing this kind of program. If you approach all your programs with urgency and importance, everyone at your property will do the same. For this particular program, it is important that the general manager be involved and support it. As an added benefit, this program is the best way to learn from and get to know some of the most talented chefs in your area. You and your staff will begin networking with some very talented people. It is all good.

THE CHEFS' TABLE

A dinner group I started a few years ago to build on the concept of learning from visiting and local chefs we call the Chefs' Table. The idea for this group came to me after a long day of writing VIP menus for member dinners, an exercise that took me all day. After finishing the tenth menu, I thought to myself, it would be nice to sit and enjoy one of these dinners myself. So I sent out letters to the top six chefs in the city, to chefs I wanted to get to know, to chefs with outstanding reputations, and—bottom line—to chefs I wanted to sit down and have dinner with. What we do is commit to five or six dinners a year; each of us takes a turn hosting the dinner. We have outstanding dinners and great wines, and we enjoy each others' company. No politics, no dues, no elections, and no business.

We have two rules: (1) if you host the event you cannot work it, you have to sit down and enjoy the evening, and (2) you must have fun and enjoy each other's company. The important thing here is to put it in the calendar. You have to schedule it, because chefs are the worst when it comes to committing and RSVPing. It is work to plan and make it happen. But it is also great to get out with your significant other and to have a wonderful evening with talented chefs. The reason I bring it up during the educational chapter is that it is a great education for you to dine with some of the best chefs in town; you will become great friends and great resources for one another. These chefs will usually be willing to do culinary demos and serve as visiting chefs for dinners at your property and for your staff. So our small, core group of seven chefs and spouses remain very loyal to each other. It is a pretty special and tight-knit group.

CONDUCT SIT-DOWNS

This is a time when I invite my employees, one at a time, to my office, and we have a sit-down. Believe it or not, my staff appreciates this effort the most. Your staff wants a piece of you, even if it is just some time for individual attention. When was the last time you took time out of your schedule to have a one-on-one with an employee? Talk about what is going on in that employee's life and background and what challenges he or she has encountered. Most of all, find out what are the goals of your employees and see what you can do to help them realize those goals—document them and hold them to it. This twenty-to-thirty-minute meeting can be the best spent time of your entire week. Your employees will appreciate this more than you know.

They will form a trust with you. One of my favorite sayings is: "What comes around goes around." Also used at end of Chapter 7, page 5. The way you lead your staff will have a huge impact on how they treat their staff, as they move up the success ladder.

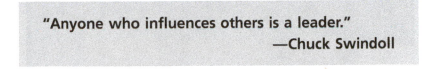

"Anyone who influences others is a leader."
—Chuck Swindoll

KEEP LOG BOOKS

Encourage your staff to maintain personal log books for each work station. These logs will become a valuable tool when they need to train someone. It is also important for keeping recipes, ratios, and menus. This is a must. Hopefully, as chefs gain experience, they will move around in the kitchen. To succeed, they should keep great records of each station so that they will have excellent, first-hand notes to support them in future positions. Every cook should look at every station, every job, as if she is the head chef of that position. They should all want that job. This is what will help them be great. I honestly believe that all my rising stars should want my job. If you continue to simply do just the job at hand, that is all you will ever do. But if you do your job every day, trying to think how your boss would think, you will excel.

MENU CHALLENGE

Pick an area on your menu you are not happy with and challenge your team to come up with five ideas to improve the situation. This forces them to study and think about the problem, and it will help you with your research. Employees are proud to have an item on the menu that they helped develop. They will also begin to bring you more and more ideas, even without you having to ask. The communication between you and your staff will be enhanced by challenging your staff to think deeply about menus and working to resolve problems.

STUDY THE CLASSICS

Post a few pages of Éscoffier's writings on starches and vegetables, and challenge your staff to use them on buffets and brunches. Make them research the classics.

Log books and recipe manuals are a great way for everyone to stay on track, be consistent, as well as invaluable resources.

GET TO KNOW YOUR SURROUNDING SCHOOLS

Maintain a good relationship with local schools so that you can recruit young aspiring chefs. Young chefs add life to your program. They ask more questions, and they make people think.

The beauty of the above educationally focused suggestions is that they did not cost you or the company any money. So there is no use for the excuse—"it cost too much." Did I teach somebody something today? If your answer to that question is no, go to the kitchen and teach at least one person something.

Money Well Spent

I have a lot more ideas for fostering the educational development of your staff, although the following programs will cost a few dollars:

- Set up an *extended exchange program* with a chef who has a busy season that is opposite of yours. In Texas we slow down in July and August, and that is when the clubs up north are the busiest. During the off-season, I arrange for some chefs to work in other resorts to gain additional experiences.

- Establish a *one-week exchange program.* Send a chef to another property to gain additional training and work experience in his or her area of expertise.

- Budget *continuing education* money for some of your key employees. This can include culinary and hospitality management courses at local schools. Oftentimes your purveyors will have two-day training programs that they will pay for members of your staff to attend. Many times the meat companies will have such programs.

- Look *for cost-effective programs in your area* that may also provide beneficial experience to your employees. We have had chocolate demos come to town that are sponsored by a pastry purveyor. Local schools often have visiting chefs, lectures, and demonstrations that they open up to the public. Local food show competitions are a great education, whether you are competing or not. Vendor shows, where suppliers set up hundreds of booths, are a good education for your staff. I have taken my staff on tours of local purveyors' warehouses to see firsthand where the product comes from. I have also taken chefs to local markets and superstores that have every vegetable available. Exposing them to something different is a great way to inspire your staff. The opportunity to get out and see something different is a valuable tool. You need to take part in these discussions to further inspire them to think. When you see a certain salad or vegetable you can elaborate with your staff where you think this product could work. Ask them their thoughts.

- *Send one of your chefs to a local restaurant to work* for a week or two. We talked earlier about the visiting chefs program. Now you have all these new friends from local properties. Ask them if one of your chefs can train at their property for a week. For me, just touring another kitchen is an education, let alone working in one for a week. This is a fantastic opportunity for your chefs to see a different style. Trust me, they will learn.

> **"Do not confuse motion and progress. A rocking horse keeps moving but does not make any progress."**
>
> **—Alfred Montapert**

Always remember, whatever you do for an individual, you will get back tenfold.

Candid Catering

A lot of the educational development ideas I've discussed so far are not new concepts to management as a whole, but they have not been ideas traditionally applied to the culinary environment. But there are also plenty of ideas that are culinary specific that I've developed over time that, I think, should become standard operating procedure for all kitchens. A fantastic tool I started in 2003 is a system I call *Candid Catering*. I wanted to start documenting all of the food we were doing for various events. Sometimes we are so busy we forget what a great menu we did two weeks ago. It's a shame we put so much time, effort, and research into great meals day after day, and often we don't do anything to preserve all of these beautiful concepts, or at least I didn't used to. Why reinvent the wheel every time? So I started cataloging all of the meals we prepared by using a digital camera, creating a photographic database. It allows the team to take a concept and to continue working with it to improve it. It really is a must. It has become a tremendous tool for the catering department.

For club business, I meet with the members five to ten times a week to plan their special events. I used to draw the plate designs in front of them; the members loved to watch me. They became somewhat mesmerized as I drew the appetizers and entrées.

As I collected all of the food pictures, I put them into files by food categories: lamb, beef, entrée salads, soups, appetizer salads, chicken, and so on. There is a great program called Picasa that can be downloaded for free from http://www.picasa.com. This program allows you to view slideshow presentations professionally. It really is great. At that point, I decided it was time to build a catering meeting room that included a flat screen and computer for presentations using this program. Now, when we have meetings with the members or guests, we dim the lights, place a small plate of warm cookies in the middle of the table, and walk through their menu.

If a member tells me he would like a four-course meal and maybe veal for the entrée. Boom—I go to the veal category, and I now mesmerize them with full-color pictures that phase in and out with the food options. We discuss adding or taking off certain items they would like to change. By demonstrating what we have done for previous events, we can better customize a new event to the member's preferences. The visual presentation allows everyone to have the best idea of the final outcome. It also greatly reduces any miscommunications.

Also included in the program are categories for centerpieces, napkin folds, ice sculptures, room set-ups, and table designs, all details guests sometimes don't think about. You really can create whatever you desire, whatever will help you sell the party.

Next, we print a quick menu and print out 8″ × 10″ photos of the meal, place them in a white folder with a gold ROCC emblem on it, and send the member on their way with a folder representation of their event. This is especially nice for brides and grooms. Often they are very excited about all of the wedding plans and like taking the photos home to show friends and family.

This has been a great tool for us. It is hard to believe that I haven't found anybody else doing this yet. I have to believe that all catering departments will eventually have to do this to stay current with all of the computer technology today. It sure does beat the old, falling apart, and outdated photo album that is found in many properties. This is a much more contemporary system that you can update weekly with ease.

Now that I have well over 1,000 images on our computer, we have all kinds of options. One option that our catering department loves and uses often is the capability to e-mail proposed menus. Many times companies or members who are doing company business will have their assistant call the club and arrange a lunch meeting. We are able to e-mail these menus and photos to them, and the lunch meeting is planned within a few minutes instead of having a one-hour, live meeting that takes the client away from work. I believe our catering department will tell you that this tool alone is worth all the work.

Another advantage to this photographic database system is that all of the dishes on the program have a text description associated with the photo. All you need to do is double-click the photo and the menu description appears at the bottom of the page. This has cut a lot of time out of my schedule, meaning that I have fewer meetings with clients, because our catering department has pictures of the food as well as a menu description. Many times the chef is needed for descriptions of the food, but in this case the work is done.

Now the last tool relevant to this concept is a plasma TV in the kitchen. Now, before all of you start accusing me of watching football on Sundays, give me a chance to explain this great concept.

As I have stated before, our club is crazy busy most of the time, with up to 70 parties a week. The opportunity to prepare something other than what members wanted or ordered is very possible based on the volume of selections and the amount of business. Photographs of all items on the day's menu are projected on the plasma screen first thing in the morning. Information on all appetizers, soups, entrées, and desserts, the time of day, the room they are to be served in, and the name of the group are displayed. Any other housekeeping notices, meeting times, upcoming events, or employee recognitions are also posted. Our one-a-day meetings are also held near the screen so that we can reference china needs, chef responsibilities,

Photos of the dishes being prepared for the day can be displayed for everyone in the kitchen to see.

and prep assignments. We also show PowerPoint slides of other foods for inspiration, visiting chef announcements, guiding principle of the week, and any other information that aids communication with the kitchen team.

It is that simple. Chances are you are already familiar with programs that help you organize your digital photos. Now simply apply the same concepts to your kitchen operation and help to organize your team. Use the work you have created already to teach your team. Additionally, your catering department will love you and your general manager will be proud of the technology you are bringing to the property, and you have an awesome chance to up-sell. When guests have an opportunity to see the food (seeing is believing), they may go the extra step and buy a little extra. And the final reason why you will love the plasma screen—drum roll, please—fewer tastings will be required. That is correct, you will need fewer tastings, because the guest can now see the food. They will trust you more because they can see it. Fewer tastings reduces time and labor.

Was It Good Enough?

Let's step back to the "ask yourself questions" concept from Chapter 1. It is important that your staff knows your passions, your standards, your drive for perfection. Let them know why you are constantly asking them to change a dish or use a different method.

We do several five-to-twelve-course VIP meals a year. So many, in fact, that I put a sous chef in charge of these events. Many times the design of the VIP dinners was proposed four to six weeks earlier. As you may have experienced, sometimes the concept written on paper does not always come out the way you had planned. If I am having a good day and am somewhat caught up, I try to go to the gym for a quick workout between 2:00 and 4:00 P.M. When I come back from the workout, I am feeling like a million bucks, all fired up, and ready to put the dinner out. As I work out, I always think about what I need to do when I get back, what can we do better, what changes can we make that would push each course over the top. (One day I came up with the brilliant idea to put sugar-wine charms on all the wine glasses for a VIP wine dinner for twenty people. You need to ask my pastry chef about that one!)

Anyway, the staff saw me coming back from a workout, and they had some of the mise-en-place for the dinner on the table. As I walked by I heard one of the chefs say, "It doesn't matter anyway, because Chef is going to change everything." I looked at the other chefs, some had smirks on their face and some didn't.

> **"I just want to make it better! It is that simple."**

You see, I did not really realize how much I change things at the last minute until someone made a joke about it. I get excited about the opportunity to make a plate better and did not really take into consideration the other chefs' work and timing. Well, okay, I did realize that it took some effort to prep a last-minute tweak for 500 people, but I just wanted it. I'm always asking myself: *Is it good enough?* So the chefs had some fun ribbing me about how I always do this, and I was okay with this, because everyone was having fun. So I apologized for making last-minute changes and explained to them why: "I just want to make it better!" It is that simple. Is it really the best we can do? Can we do something better, can we add something? And don't abandon the concept that sometimes making a plate better means taking something off. So after we talked about it, it became a game. *"What is he thinking, what is he going to make us do?"* At this point the team is inspired, as they start thinking for themselves and trying to stay a step ahead of me. That is when you can see growth, when they start thinking like you.

Use this as a tool. Make it one of your guiding principles. "Improve everything we touch!" I love that one. I have found that many times in competition or at work, when designing plates, our first design is usually pretty good. You have to be careful not to accept "good." It is amazing how a "good" plate design turns into a great plate when *everyone* is constantly thinking, "what if," and we try this or do that. That is a great way to start out a sentence by the way, "What if...?" Make sure you talk to all your staff about this, and be sure you instill the *desire to be challenged.* If they understand it, they will be vested into the system. They will want to be part of the design phase. They will say and feel: "Hey, I have a vote."

"Improve everything we touch."

So the next time an employee brings you an idea, recipe, or plate, you can say—"That is great, Chef. What do you think we can do to make it better?" As long as they understand the objective, they will appreciate the question. This is a great educational tool and will have a fantastic influence on your kitchen environment.

One last thought on education. I think young people new to cooking have to be careful. I have seen cooks working the line who never have given a thought to what should be their next step. Some have been doing the same job for fifteen to twenty years, and they are good at it. Problem is, they don't have much to retire on. I think cooks can easily slide into a bad pattern fast, if they are not focused.

"Ask yourself the question, 'What if...?'"

Cooks often work in a restaurant before going to culinary school to get a taste of what it is like. These are young cooks right out of high school, some hanging out after a late shift of working the line; they stay up late, possibly indulging in adult beverages, get up the next day, and do it all over again. Finally, these young chefs go to culinary school, graduate, and go into an entry level position, working the line, getting out of work late (wound up), then going out with their fellow cooks. They are wearing the same jacket they wore before they went to school and following the same pattern; the whole scene is the same. Cooks have to be careful with the transition from college to their first job out of school, or they could waste valuable time fooling around. The first day of the rest of a young cook's life has just started, whether he or she is ready or not!

Consider a broker, lawyer, doctor, advertising professional, or any professional field, when these students graduate and then walk into their first job at the firm (or wherever), the "first day of the rest of their life just started." They have a suit on, their game face is on, and they know they need to start growing up fast. I think there is a more defined "change" in these peoples lives as opposed to a chef's life. The pay is much different as well. Corporations can afford to take on a brilliant graduate for anywhere from $50,000 to $100,000 a year, whereas a newly graduated cook may have to start out at $12 an hour. Because our industry just cannot pay that kind of money we can only charge so much for a cup of coffee. Our young people have to be truly focused on their career if they are going to be successful. We have to help them understand the road to success.

Without doing any research, I believe that a student graduating into the culinary industry is probably one of the lowest paid. For this reason, there should be a lot of guidance for our young people, so they do not make bad decisions. Yes, they will get paid little to start; but if they take the right roads, they too can eventually be paid incredibly well. We need to help them realize their goals, find out what it is they want to do with their education, help them find the best people in our industry in that particular category, and steer them in the direction of their success. If they carefully map out their future, they will excel and make an impact on our industry. But we have to help.

As chefs, we should do everything we can to steer young people in the direction to focus on their future.

Chapter 9

Fostering Success

As I stated in the last chapter, chefs should be willing and eager to do what they can to steer new chefs in the direction of success. Fostering the success of other chefs can be accomplished in many different ways, including mentoring and helping chefs to develop a work ethic.

Establish a Framework for Success

It is sad that in this day and age to be considered a "pretty good" employee is to do what someone asks of you. We are expected to be satisfied when someone actually completes the task he or she is asked to do. When did just getting by become acceptable?

Young people should want to excel, and they can begin to excel by doing one simple thing:

COMPLETE every job asked of you better than your boss expected it to be done! It is the first step toward becoming great. Our world is polluted with below-standard performances. If you want to set yourself apart from the rest, if you want to succeed, to grow, to get promoted, and to be great, just do the following:

> **"Complete every job asked of you better than it was expected."**

One of the goals of this book is to help set up a framework for all who are reading this, all who wish to excel, to be promoted, to climb the ladder, and one day to be a true team leader and executive chef. In fact, this secret is for everyone who has a boss and wants to become a boss.

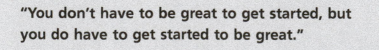

> **"You don't have to be great to get started, but you do have to get started to be great."**

Our mentality should be to think like our bosses, to think better than our bosses. When your boss asks something of you, you complete it better than he or she ever could imagine. If your boss is about to grab something, strive to have what he or she is reaching for. Anticipate the needs of your boss, staying one step ahead. If you stay ahead of your boss, you can start thinking of what needs to be done, what needs improvement, thinking of ways *to do it better!* Don't wait to be told what to do. Think as an individual; think as a chef, not as an apprentice. Remember, you have to pretend to be something before you can actually become it. If you sit back and wait to be told everything, you will not excel. Chew off the end of the table if needed. Want it. Complete jobs in such a way that the boss has *no choice but to promote you.* Leave no cards on the table. Your work ethic should be so powerful, so admirable, so thorough that you make an *impact.* Be influential! Be someone whose work ethic is so strong that you make the chefs around you work harder. These people, I guarantee, get promoted! You don't have to be great to get started, but you have to get started to be great.

Mentoring

The power of helping people comes from making an impact on someone's life! The responsibilities of a mentor are enormous, both in effort and by example. Leading by example is really only the first formula for success.

Webster's dictionary defines a mentor as a wise and trusted teacher, guide, and friend. There you have it. Pretty black and white, wouldn't you agree? A wise and trusted teacher, guide, and friend. But sometimes I think the word mentor is used a little too freely. Just because you got someone a job or gave someone a word of advice, does not necessarily make you a mentor.

> **"No person was ever honored for what he received. Honor has been the reward for what he gave."**
>
> **—Calvin Coolidge**

I remember talking to a restaurateur who claimed to have mentored a media chef I happened to know. The restaurant owner said that this chef trained with him. One day I was talking to this famous chef and asked him about his experience with this person. He said he worked at the restaurant for three months and had to leave because he did not agree with some of the sanitation practices. It is funny how the story gets changed around depending on who you talk to. Mentoring is a responsibility; it is not a short-term job.

I sincerely believe that huge responsibility goes along with being a mentor. The end result of giving, helping, mentoring, and making a difference in someone's life is beyond and better than any award or trophy. If you have been a mentor and your protégé has moved on successfully, they are a part of you. Their standard of excellence is a reflection of you.

Who do you admire the most, professionally and personally? What do you admire about them and why? Why do you want to be like this person? What do they do that makes you want to be like them? This is yet another opportunity to ask yourself pointed questions. Once you determine why you admire someone—do what they do! Put yourself and your staff in the best situation to succeed. You have heard interviews with coaches after games. How many times have you heard a coach say, "It's my job to put the best combination of players on the field that will give us the best chance to win." That is also the job of the chef, of any leader.

Have you ever studied or watched Tiger Woods walk off a green and proceed to the next hole? Have you ever noticed how focused he is? Thousands of people line up within three feet of him just to get close to the champion. Some try to get autographs, but you never see him stop during a round to sign. He is already thinking about where on the next fairway he wants to hit his next shot and then what iron he plans to hit with after that. If he were to stop and get caught up with the crowd, he would lose his focus. How many shots ahead are you thinking? Maybe you are still admiring the shot you hit two holes ago. What would happen if you, as a chef, focused and practiced like Tiger Woods? What would happen if kids today practiced liked Tiger Woods?

Work Ethic

Why change if you don't need to change? Why do you need to change as long as you are happy, put food on the table, clothe yourself, and appear successful? Why try to do better?

> **"You miss 100 percent of the shots you never take."**
>
> **—Wayne Gretzky**

I was on a plane not too long ago and overheard a gentleman talk about his son, a senior in high school. In the course of his conversation, he made one comment that really bothered me. He stated that his son only had to go to school until 9:30 A.M., because he had all the credits he needed to graduate. He was talking about how he had to mow the lawn, because he could not get his boy to stop watching television long enough to mow it. I felt very sad for some reason. What a waste. Would this be acceptable to you? What signals are we giving our children if we let them quit when it is just good enough, when they do just enough to get by, and then go home and watch television. If the kid was going to some kind of senior work-in-the-industry plan where some kids start working in a field in which they are interested, I could accept this. But he was watching television. The young man will never get his senior year back. He will never get that chance to do a little extra, to grab another course that could better prepare him for life. That year is gone. And you know what, it is really not all his fault. In fact, in my opinion, most of it is not his fault. I would blame the parents more than the child. What has happened to our younger generations? If my dad told me to sweep the street, I swept the street—no questions asked. That is what you did when your parents asked you to do something. It seems that the younger generations have changed. Dr. Rick Rigsby has a great book called *Lessons from a Third Grade Dropout* (Nashville, TN: Nelson Ignite, 2006) in which he describes very well what separates the generations. It truly is a great book.

Your Work Ethic Defines You

This begs the question: Is *good* good enough? I will share with you my fear: when someone decides that the product you serve does not stand up to the expensive hotel down the street and when your styles are getting old and guests would rather go to the property with a new chef with great new ideas. Are you giving your all to your property?

> **"If no one ever took risks, Michelangelo would have painted the Sistine floor."**
> **—Neil Simon, playwright**

Currently, River Oaks Country Club is having a record-breaking year. Every single month over the past ten months, it has broken food sales numbers for that month. Last January (2006) was the busiest January in the club's history. We have broken the records for eleven straight months. This is really an incredible statistic. I credit our record-breaking sales to the $13 million-dollar renovation—we are all new, and the economy is on an upswing. The reason I am telling you this is because I could have taken a fat vacation this past summer, relied on how good business has been, and depended on the fact that we put out a pretty good product. The year was a chef's dream, with all numbers fantastic—so sit back, get fat, relax, and enjoy the ride. Wrong.

I knew we were riding a horse, as it were, and eventually the horse would slow down. So while we were breaking records, I spent the slow months designing all new banquet stations and researching new display china and layouts. I reworked the banquet menus as well as the packages that presented all new events. In short, I focused on continuing to re-create ourselves. My goal is to set the standard and push to be the best at what we do. If you don't do this as well, if you don't have this attitude, you will be passed by. Don't get too comfortable. Don't catch yourself admiring your last shot for too long. Be more concerned about the next two holes and what you plan to do to make them. Destiny is a choice not a chance.

Some of you are sitting there thinking: "I don't get paid anywhere near enough to possibly put in any more hours." Let me share with you something that happened to me not so long ago. I had noticed the declining attitude of one of my cooks over a two-month period. He was constantly angry and often snapped at people when spoken to. His production was great some days but not so great other days. I finally scheduled a sit-down with him to try to find out what was bothering him. I asked "Rob" how he was doing. He replied "fine," with some reserve, not really understanding why he was in my office. I told him I had noticed an extreme decline in his attitude and production lately and wanted to know if there was something bothering him. I could tell he was very uncomfortable; then he started talking:

"To be honest chef, I am not happy. I have been wanting a position, and I keep getting passed over for it. And I want a raise. I work hard. Why can't I get a raise?"

Now this was shaping up to be an interesting conversation. So I asked Rob if he thought his work performance had been less than stellar over the past six months.

"Yes I guess it has, sure it has. I have not been very happy about my position or the money."

I responded, "So let me get this straight. You are not happy about your job; you want to get promoted? You feel you have been doing unacceptable work; yet you want a raise. Have I got it right?"

Rob had a puzzled, frustrated facial expression.

"Rob, what would you do if you were me?"

"Chef, I see what you are saying. But why can't I get promoted? You know I want this job."

"Would you give it to *you*, if you were *me?* You're asking me to promote and to give someone a raise who has been underperforming and angry."

Rob continued to be frustrated.

At this point I started to explain to Rob what I had seen over the past few months. He agreed with me on my evaluation and wanted to do something about it, but he did not really know where to start.

"What would you say your attitude and work performance needs to be to warrant a raise and promotion?" I asked.

You see it all comes back to asking the right questions and, more importantly, once you get the answer, doing something with it. Do something with the information you just learned, act on it. Once you have the answers, use them to improve and motivate yourself. Information is absolutely useless unless you put it into effect. Use the lesson, putting the answer into practice 110 percent will help you grow. It is like a computer or the forms I have talked about in this book. You can put all the information into a computer or onto a form, but if you don't turn the computer on or act on the information on the forms, neither will help you.

We need to get to the bottom of what was really affecting Rob's work performance and then act on correcting it.

There Is No Substitute for Experience

I know the pain and worry of many thousand-dollar bills from school. I know how it feels to have such an unfathomable debt before you even get your first job. I understand as a new professional that there is a need, an anxiety, a desire to *have* money *now* to start paying off those bills.

And then there is the eager, very talented culinarian who believes that he or she is equipped to be executive chef directly out of school. There are also the individuals who do pick up skills quickly and want to be promoted immediately or moved to another station *now,* because in their minds, they have learned everything they need and don't need that station anymore. It is time to move on.

Time and again I run up against such mentalities. Many times a young person really does not want to hear anything others have to say unless it has something to do with a promotion, more money, embroidered jackets, or black supervisor pants. There is a difference between entitlement and the drive to succeed. I want young chefs to *want* to excel. They need to have the drive, but it is the responsibility of experienced chefs to harness that drive so they can be successful.

How many times have you heard about a fantastic, incredibly talented college athlete who did not make it in the big leagues? I'm talking about athletes who have every resource thrown at them to be successful, who have all the talent in the world in their hands, who are chosen by many to be among the all-time greats in the game, and who then fail. What happened to these athletes? Did they not use the endless resources available to them? Did they choose not to listen to all of the counseling offered to them? Did they allow drugs, unlawful acts, wrong decisions, or bad influences to steer them? Did they think they had all the answers instead of listening to the experienced mentor's recommendations? I watched a segment on television a few years ago about Leon Spinks, one of the best professional boxers ever to come up through the ranks. He became heavyweight champion of the world. He is now pushing a broom in a local high school, working as a janitor. What happened in his life to go from top-level success in his chosen career to such a low point and out of the game?

DOES YOUR CAREER HAVE FOCUS?

My point is that there are thousands of disaster stories of wasted talent in the world. Because these individuals were not able to focus on their career goals and the factors involved in gaining and maintaining success, because they were not patient enough to get the proper experience needed to reach greatness, failure is the most common result. There is no substitution for experience, period! Yes, I became executive chef at a very young age; but it did not happen until I had worked in all departments of the resort for a minimum of a year. My goal was to learn more about each department than the department heads themselves. I then went to culinary school, completed my externship, returned to the resort, became a sous chef and executive sous chef, and *then* I became executive chef. Six years learning everything I could and seven years as executive chef shows a pretty solid commitment in my mind.

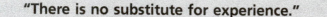

"There is no substitute for experience."

FIND THE OPPORTUNITIES

To be successful you can't always go for the "low-hanging fruit." Looking for that forty-thousand-dollar-a-year job directly out of school may not be the best step for you. It is a challenge for an experienced chef to make a young person understand this.

So many times young chefs come to me and want to move on or move out, because they are bored with the station where they are working. In many cases, in my opinion, the chef is missing the obvious opportunity. Do they know everything about that station? Have they proven that they can run that station without any assistance? Or, better yet, can they lead other chefs in that department?

I care deeply for the success of all my chefs, especially the young spitfires who have so much talent. But there is nothing that saddens me more than when I see them make a decision that, in my heart, I know is not the right one. I try to explain to them that I care about their future and can help them be successful over the next two to four years, whether it be at my property or a colleague's property that better fits their needs.

The first step is always the hardest: getting them to listen. They just want somebody to show them the money. They need to find out what it is they want to accomplish in their career, find out who are considered the best at it, and then do what they do. They need to research success stories. I always make a point of telling newer chefs that the success of the people they admire did not happen in just a few years time. The most successful chefs spent years honing their skills, learning from others, and gaining experience before reaching their current levels of success.

We live in a society where everybody wants it right now. Instant gratification. It is difficult to wait for your success to blossom. The culinary pay scale is probably one of the most difficult challenges in our industry today. A chef has to dedicate so much time and effort into development and gaining experience before he or she can start making a substantial amount of money.

If you take only one thing away from reading this book, it should be this: If you cheat your time to gain valuable experience, you will cheat your payday later in your career. I guarantee it. You get back what you put in, so if you don't put much into gaining the necessary experience, you will not accomplish your ultimate goals and will not be paid accordingly for your success.

Work every job to get the best reference possible. Imagine receiving this as a reference from a reputable chef:

> She is such a great professional chef. She is going to be a fantastic executive chef one day. Her follow-through and attitude only make those around her want to be better. She completes all jobs better than I could have asked for, her preparation before and after a work shift is unprecedented. She has volunteered for anything needed in the kitchen and has studied in all departments on her own time. She will always have a home and a job in Texas.

The chef who received this reference now has gained all the resources of the chef who provided the reference. Is it really that difficult to understand? You can't pay for that kind of knowledge and experience; you can only earn it establishing and following through on your work ethic. With one or two other references like the one above, who do you think will be most successful—the chef who cheated himself of this time or the chef who actually put the work into it?

Ask yourself the following question: If you could trade five years of your life after graduating from a culinary school to gain fifty years of prestigious chefs' recommendations, connections, and resources, would you? That the answer is a resounding yes is a no-brainer. It is all an investment for your career and your future. To be successful in any career, you need the shared experience of the work itself and those around you.

> **"Invest in your own future!"**
> **"Don't cheat yourself!"**

Make an Impact!

Make an impact. Decide you want to do something special with your life. Do it with 110 percent of your effort.

Chapter 10

How to Get People to Want to Work for You

How Do You Get People to Want to Work for You?

This is a great question, and accomplishing it can be an art form. As a young professional, this is something you want to work on early in your career. The answer is *respect*. Treat people with respect, and they will respect you. The secret to receiving respect is that you have to respect yourself before you can respect anybody else. Next, *empower* your employees to do the right thing, to make the right decision, and in return you must show them you trust them. You have to trust your experts in each of your departments. You are not in the trenches doing their job, they are. Don't pretend to have all the answers. Do you? It is not possible. Hopefully, you hire great people who can add their opinions and experiences to the overall goal of producing the best product. I always ask all of my staff, in each department, for their opinions. We *all* listen to *all* the ideas, and then we choose which direction to go. Most importantly, for success, once we agree on the answer, we all support it, period.

1. Give respect to receive respect.
2. Respect is a great influence on job performance.
3. Receiving respect builds confidence.
4. Don't dismiss new ideas and certainly not complaints. Learn more about new ideas and complaints to make an informed decision.

I once had a cook who constantly complained to me that he did not have enough kitchen utensils to do his job and that he was losing valuable time every day because of it. I disagreed with the cook and told him that he shouldn't be afraid to wash a spoon or two. Once I had to work his station, during the middle of the night, I found I was short of all kinds of equipment I thought the station needed. Long story short, the next week the cook had the equipment he needed and more. Get in there and find out for yourself. Listen to your staff.

HOW CLEAN IS YOUR KITCHEN?

You might be wondering why I am talking about sanitation in this section but bear with me. Are you proud to give guest tours of your kitchen, whether to guests or a visiting chef? Is it sparkling clean? If not, why not? Is the standard not high enough? Do your employees not care, or do they think they don't have to clean because you have a stewarding team or a night cleaning crew? Be sure you instill high standards in your team when it comes to cleaning. Make sure they all know that they are responsible for sweeping, mopping, and scrubbing the stoves according to schedule.

Are changes being made to your kitchen or property? Make sure to give your input and do not be afraid to ask your staff's opinion, after all, they are working the station.

There are four things I have done each time I have taken a new job. There have been some jobs where I did not want the public to know I was hired until I could get the kitchen clean enough to meet my standards. If guests know a new chef has started, they expect the food to be all new that first day. But it takes time to implement changes, and it can't be done on the first day. Here are my four primary rules for starting a new job:

1. Get in and clean EVERYTHING!
2. Check the lighting in the kitchen.
3. Improve the employee meal.
4. Make sure the staff has clean, professional uniforms.

Now these rules may seem strange to you, but they have been very important to me and have become operating standards for me. The rules begin to establish my standards to the rest of the staff. They begin to learn about my expectations and the importance I place on the kitchens' physical environment. And the good news is, these are changes you can plan before you even start the job. You don't have to analyze for very long to know you need to clean or that the lighting is bad.

CLEAN KITCHEN

If your kitchen is not clean, you know you have to get it done. Some properties where I have worked did not have an outside cleaning crew. I used to have "Team Days" once a month when the kitchen was closed. We ordered pizza and soda for the crew, and we cleaned everything from top to bottom, pulling everything away from the walls and giving it all a good scrub. If nothing else, this exercise makes the chefs respect how they leave the equipment at the end of their shift.

Set your standards so high that you are proud to give tours to anybody at any time of day. I don't care how old your kitchen is; there is no excuse. I have worked in kitchens that were fifty years old, and they can be kept just as clean as a brand new kitchen. And if your kitchen is extra clean...*people will want to work for you!*

LIGHTING

Whether at home or work, poor lighting is a pet peeve of mine. I have always been very sensitive to how well a room is lit. At home I like the lighting a certain way in the dining room when eating, a certain way in the living room when watching TV, and a certain way outside at night while unwinding with a great red wine. Lighting is important; it sets the mood, whatever the mood may be. In the kitchen, lighting hugely influences how our employees work

A place for everything and everything in its place.

and how our food looks. Did you know that there are hundreds of different kinds of lights available? In kitchens, it is important that a tomato looks like a tomato. And when you slice into a prime rib, you need to be able to tell that it is rare and not gray.

Fluorescent lighting is not the best presentation for food, yet most kitchens have fluorescent lighting. To get the best out of your lighting have a light consultant evaluate and recommend what is best based on your kitchen layout, design, and needs. Some kitchens are lucky enough to have natural lighting, which changes the atmosphere entirely. If you ever get a chance to build a kitchen, fight, scratch, and claw to get natural lighting in the kitchen. You will not believe the difference. Now if you have a great working environment, clean and lit like a sunny day, *people will want to work in your kitchen!*

The third week on the job at River Oaks, I relamped the entire kitchen and added two more light panels. You should have seen the difference in the kitchen and on the employees' faces when they came back to work. It was as if a weight was lifted off their shoulders. They could not believe it. They thought we put a whole new ceiling and light system in. You have to trust me on this, if you are not familiar with the effect of good lighting. The sad thing is, I have seen many kitchens so poorly lit and nobody really notices because they have been working in that environment for years. Once you get great lighting, it will drive you crazy not to have great lighting in other areas of your life.

FAMILY MEAL

Those of you who provide a family meal, or employee meals, know that the company's employees can often be more demanding than your guests. My club serves around three hundred employee meals a day, from front office executives, assistants, and managers to front-line employees, as well as people from outside departments. Along with the vast departments, we have a melting pot of ethnicities. It is sometimes challenging to please so many people and to provide them with their favorite things to eat.

On top of these challenges, we have budget constraints: cost of food, labor, and time to prepare the meals. Many operations have to provide the meal with whoever is working in the kitchen at the time. The fortunate properties have a cook and some helpers dedicated to the employee meal. Chances are most employee dining can be improved. If you first move into a job and make an effort to improve employee dining, employees will take notice and appreciate your attention to them. They will appreciate that employee food was top on your list of things to improve. Now if you care about your employees and make an effort to improve their day with a healthy, wholesome, and fresh meal, *they will want to work harder for you!*

UNIFORMS

I have always been a stickler for uniforms. I believe you have to look like a chef before you can be one. You have to act like a chef, work clean like a chef, and practice being a chef, before you can become a chef. You don't have to know what you are doing to look good! Image is very important. My

"You work like you feel."

—John Carroll

My first week at a property, I was talking to one of the managers about the chef uniforms. Baseball hats, sneakers, and mixed-matched uniforms aren't my style. I was explaining to him how important it was to me that we have professional uniforms so that everyone could feel good about themselves and feel proud to be a chef. As I was explaining my position, the manager had a smile on his face. I asked him why he was sporting the grin, and he said some of the cooks were embarrassed to wear their uniforms outside of work. "What?" I said. I'm not sure if they were embarrassed to be a chef or of the uniforms.

Obviously, I ordered new uniforms for the crew. I also awarded the employees who have been with the company for many years with their own monogrammed jackets with their titles, if they had one. It is funny, the younger you are, the more important having your name and title on the jacket is. The older you get, the less important the titles or jackets are, at least for me.

dad always used to say: "You work like you feel." So, how do you feel? What is the image you are projecting? If your guests could see the chefs who are preparing their meals, would they be happy to eat the food? It is always refreshing to me to walk into a kitchen of professionals.

Believe it or not, you have to teach people to work clean. You have to practice to be clean. You can't just wake up one morning and say—I am going to work clean today. It does not work that way. Chefs can't wipe their hands on their apron, lift pots against their chef jackets, use their aprons for side towels, use their side towels to wipe down stations, and expect to look clean and crisp. How many times have you seen a cook wipe off a table onto the floor? That drives me nuts! In reality, it really doesn't take much effort to do the right thing.

There are college football teams whose tradition is not putting names on the back of the football jerseys. Their philosophy is that the game is much bigger than any one player...something to be said about that. Make the investment to buy nice uniforms for your staff, complete with logos on the jackets. Make sure your uniform company is laundering them correctly. I have spent countless hours with laundry companies to be sure our uniforms were properly starched. It is important. In fact, when interviewing for a new job, tell the interviewer that your taking the job is contingent on getting all new uniforms for the staff, if needed. You want to bring a level of professionalism to the table. The employees should be proud of the work they do, proud of the product they put out, proud of their team, and most of all proud to be a chef! The general manager will enjoy your professionalism much more during the interview than he will when he gets the bill for the uniforms. If you provide a clean atmosphere, quality uniforms, and a professional look, *your staff will want to be professional and want to work for you!*

This Is Just the Start

These are just the very first things I attack when starting a new job, usually during the first three weeks. Obviously, there are many more challenges and issues to worry about. The reason I am spending so much time on these issues is because they all have to do with the kitchen atmosphere! And the atmosphere is one of the greatest influences on how people work. A clean kitchen, proper lighting, employee meals, and uniforms are all issues you can address during the first three weeks on the job, and these areas have a huge influence on the performance and image of your operation. That you will make nice food, create better menus, crunch better numbers, etc., is expected. But how good are you going to be if your staff hates the working environment?

Now you have all the tools necessary to get people to want to work for you. If you build the Taj Mahal of kitchen team building, educational pro-

Insist on a professional atmosphere and professional dress in your kitchen.

grams, and the best working environment, the best people will want to work for you. "If you build it, they will come." So the answer is in everything you have just read. Build it, build the educational environment, and they will come. Trust me; there are not a lot of properties with all of the above. Make it a priority to take care of your employees.

Chapter 11

Hire Right the First Time

Now that you have established what your working environment will be, it is important to get the right people in the door. As I mentioned before, if you are not offering anything other than a wage, you will only get people who punch in and punch out for their paycheck. To hire right the first time, you have to offer something to potential employees, something that makes this job more valuable than others they may be considering. And it is important that those advantages are communicated to the applicant both when the job is advertised and when the interview takes place. I think people will quit people, before they will quit their job.

> **"I have made a pledge to myself that we are only going to hire culinarians."**

1. Determine what type of person you want in the open position.
2. Don't compromise what you're looking for.
3. Hire smart!
4. Only hire dedicated culinarians.

I have made a pledge to myself that we are only going to hire dedicated culinarians. That is a big promise. Stay true to your promise. I know we have all been in the same boat when we cannot find a good employee, especially during prime season, and we start to consider hiring someone just to fill the position. I've held a position open for several weeks, waiting for the perfect fit. It is not always easy, but it is well worth the wait once you get that person. If you hire out of haste, you will pay in the long run with constant turnover, or you may even get into a situation where it is difficult to get rid of the person, not to mention the cost of hiring, training, uniforms, and paperwork. Bad hires tend to stay around and detract from the environment you are trying to build.

Job Descriptions

First, you need to have a clear idea of what you want the person to do. If you don't have job descriptions for your staff, you really need them. You need them to give applicants an accurate description of the job responsibilities. You also need them for employee reviews and as a tool for when you are having performance problems. If you don't already have job descriptions, this may seem like a lot of work. If you have a human resource department, they can help you. You can also go online and find generic descriptions and formats that will give you a good place to start, and from there you can customize the descriptions to your operation. Another method is to ask your employees to write down everything they do from the minute they walk in the door until they leave. A couple of good Web sites you can use for creating job descriptions include: www.entrepreneur.com/humanresources/hiring/article56490.html and www.toolkit.cch.com/text/P05_0300.asp.

1. Create job descriptions if you don't already have them.
2. Encourage applicants to ask questions about the job description so they fully understand job responsibilities.
3. Make sure your existing employees have a copy of their job description.
4. Make job descriptions available to employees on request, so they understand the responsibilities of other positions they are working to achieve some day.
5. Use the job description as a tool during employees' annual reviews.

Invest in the Hiring Procedure

I used to be the worst with the hiring procedure until I finally got my act together. If I was down a person, I would just hire someone and throw the individual into the kitchen mix. How can people feel a job is special if this is how they are treated? Again, your leadership team can help here. Get them involved in the process. If you get them involved in the process, the culinary team's pride will be evident in the kitchens when applicants receive their tours. My leadership team not only gets involved with the property tour and interview process, but they also helped develop the Culinary Orientation Packet (discussed below). Your people want to be involved, let them. Empower your employees to be part of the process.

> "You've got to have great athletes to win, I don't care who the coach is. You can't win without good athletes, but you can lose with them. This is where coaching makes the difference."
>
> —Lou Holtz, football coach

All properties are proud of something. Whether it is the club house, golf course, grounds, tennis program, kids' program, aquatics, kitchen or culinary program, there is something very special about all properties. In my opinion, it is vitally important that all job applicants have an opportunity to see the entire property and everything it has to offer. It informs their perspective on the job they will be doing. How can someone be excited about being a part of something they have never seen? Other than their work environment, what other area of the property have they seen? Do they understand the property's culture? I am spoiled and fortunate that River Oaks Country Club (ROCC) is incredibly endowed in all areas and the facilities are all newly renovated.

There are two things I did to make sure all employee candidates knew the scope of ROCC's offerings.

CULINARY ORIENTATION PACKET (COP)

The packet includes the following materials:

- ROCC Mission Statement
- Welcome letter from Executive Chef

- ROCC Guiding Principles
- Descriptions of:
  - Gold Card Program
  - Top Gun Award
  - Most Valuable Culinarian Awards (MVC)
  - Workout Sessions
  - Green Beret Sous-Chef Program
  - Distinguished Visiting Chef Program
- Biographies and photos of Leadership Team
- ROCC Culinary Team press releases
- Endorsements from past Green Beret candidates
- History of ROCC

I am very proud of my team and everything they have accomplished on and off the job. I am partial, but this packet is pretty impressive. When a new candidate comes to an interview, we hand them this information in a white folder with a gold logo on the cover. We either scare them to death, or they cannot wait to join the team—or a little of both. Every candidate experiences a quick glimpse into what we are all about, and then they go on a complete property tour.

PROPERTY TOUR

Once the candidate has filled out an application, the leadership team member with the job opening greets the candidate and takes them on a tour of the property. First stop is the all new, $2-million-dollar golf maintenance and grounds department. This is an impressive facility, and I think it is important for all potential employees to see all that is involved in keeping the grounds and golf course in incredible condition. Next stop is a new, state-of-the-art golf teaching facility complete with computers, plasma televisions, and cameras to help improve the golfer's swing. Next stop is the tennis stadium, home to the oldest clay-court tennis invitational in the world, the pro shop, pool area, and finally the entire clubhouse and the four kitchens. Three sous chefs are also involved with the tour, each able to talk intelligently on all aspects of the property, not just the kitchens. They also talk about all of the awards the culinary team has won. At the same time, the sous chefs get an opportunity to interview the candidate in a more casual setting. When you see the entire property, it is something everyone can be proud of, and it shows the new candidate how passionate we are about our club, while at the same time giving us a chance to learn more about the candidate. The tour ends in my office, and I conduct a final interview.

The First Day of Work

On the first day of work, the new employee finalizes all paperwork with human resources, views safety videos, and becomes acquainted with the employee laundry system. As well, the employee is introduced to the facility's general manager, among others. After all this, the employee begins cross training with the sous chef of the particular department for which he or she was hired.

Culinary Certificate

After an employee is hired, we recognize the individual in front of the full staff at the first workout session the new employee attends and present to him or her a beautiful Team Certificate, worthy of framing. I am fortunate in that I usually have a small list of people wanting to get into the program. This is very special for me, and I want to be sure that I live up to their expectations.

Once You Have Hired, Retain

As we all know, employee retention is not something the culinary world has done very well. My approach is simple. Organize yourself. SEF: Schedule, Empower, and Follow Up. Sit down with your new employees, go over their job descriptions, and share your goals for them. Talk about the goals they have set for themselves. Give them something to reach for and help them reach it. Over the years, I have been blessed with some talented cooks and chefs. The past six years we have seen a chef per year leave and move on to a first executive chef position.

We rarely lose young cooks once they start the program. The Journeyman Program, the latest from the Product Champion's program, is currently being developed to consistently rotate all our young chefs through all the departments. This will be hugely successful for our kitchen and the young chefs, as it constantly provides an educational environment and keeps our sous chefs sharp, because they are always teaching.

The Best Are Typically the First

Isn't it true that typically your best employees are the first to go? What does that leave you with? Unfortunately, it is usually the employees you want to go that stay with you. Maybe, maybe not. Obviously, your superstars and overachievers are working hard toward promotion, and eventually they leave

Putting effort into the retention of employees is invaluable.

for their first executive chef positions. Throughout this book, I have been encouraging everyone to step up, to want to do better, to excel, and to get that first executive chef job. That many executive chefs do not want their sous chefs to move on is unfortunate but understandable. It takes too long to get good help and too long to train good people. How many times have you, as executive chef, received a call about potential candidates for an available entry-level chef's position and had someone who was ready but did not tell the young chef about the opportunity? I am guessing that this happens a lot in our industry. It is understandable that you would not want to lose an "A" player, but I will share with you an idea that may help you with this.

Always be on the lookout for your next sous chef. You never know when you will need a great employee, and you know they are difficult to come by. I know all too well that our labor budgets are tight, and we cannot just hire at will, so what do you do? Inspire! Inspire your employees; make an impact with your sous-chef team. When you identify this next sous-chef candidate, explain the value of your teaching program and how you may not be able to pay immediately the candidate's full worth, but if he or she works hard for you, great things will happen. In addition, assure your candidate that you will prepare him or her for an executive chef position. To provide this training, I developed the Green Beret Sous-Chef Program.

> **"Throw your heart over the bar, and your body will follow."**
>
> —Advice from a veteran trapeze artist

Green Beret Sous-Chef Program

The Green Beret Sous-Chef Program at River Oaks Country Club was created to help train, mentor, motivate, and prepare eager culinarians to achieve their first executive chef positions. These candidates successfully hold all the sous-chef positions at the ROCC, and the program culminates with the candidates' operation of the Grill Restaurant. During the sous-chef experience, all aspects of the country club are learned. They are required to attend house committee meetings (a member-led committee that oversees anything to do with the inside of a club, particularly with food and beverage provision) and menu-planning meetings for member functions. They also must be a member of the leadership team and be involved with budgeting, scheduling, and overall aspects of running a successful club as executive chef.

We aid in the preparation of the chef and assist in his or her placement by researching potential properties and assisting in the negotiation of salary and benefit packages. Overall, this program benefits everyone—the chef is properly trained and fostered into a new position with all aspects carefully attended to and set up for success. The property hiring the new executive chef gets a solid candidate with a great leadership and culinary background. And, as new positions open up at River Oaks Country Club, more culinarians are given the opportunity to excel, to be promoted, and to visualize their own self-growth.

The first time one of our sous chefs moved on to his first big job, the rest of the staff stood at attention. They see the process in full; they see that if they work hard and push for their own success, they too can be successful. Sometimes you can almost see a light go off in their heads that says, "Hey, I don't have to be a line cook all my life." I love young kitchens because they are full of life, full of spirit. There are not a lot of kitchens in the United States that help their sous chefs move on to their next jobs. They cannot be bothered. It takes too long to train a good sous chef, and they are too hard to come by.

Again, the secret here is to...guess? *Schedule it.* Plan, with your sous chefs, to prepare them for the next step. Tell them that you will help them get to the next level if they help you. You work on the sous chef's goals together. This is vitally important. If you both understand the goals and the timeline, you can help each other. You have time to bring in another sous chef to cross train and the outgoing sous chef has time to land the perfect job with your recommendation and full support.

Are you willing to push your employees beyond their comfort zones in order to achieve excellence? To help them achieve excellence? Hopefully, they will respect you for it, and if they don't, something tells me that they will one day. One day when they have a boss who does not push them, who is satisfied with just being good, someone who doesn't challenge employees to greatness, then they will appreciate what you did for them.

Termination

A little bit of a sour subject, but we should talk about it. What is the proper way to terminate? Fifteen years ago the procedure was not as strict as it is now. Human resources is a huge part of what we do as chefs. How we act, how we talk, how our staff talks, what we allow to happen or stop from happening is the responsibility of the executive chef. This is serious business nowadays. If you allow certain attitudes to continue in your kitchen that are negative, abusive, or harassing, whether you are involved or not, you can be held liable along with the company.

So, when employees leave the property, what is the procedure? What should we do as employers, as executive chef of the kitchen, during the termination? First, I like to ask a few questions.

Exit Interview

Arrange an exit interview with the employee who is leaving, whether it is a termination or a resignation. You need this opportunity to find out some key information that you can learn from and possibly use to improve your operation. Document your questions. Create a form that includes questions that are important to you. For me, the following questions are a good start:

- Why are you leaving?
- Are you unhappy with the job, or are you taking the next step in a job?
- How has the experience been at the club?

- Would you change anything at the club?
- Do you have any issues with the current operation?

Ask questions! It is always the best way to get an answer, right? As you know, my philosophy on this technique is that it is okay not to have all the answers, but it *not* okay just to sit back and not ask the right questions. You learn by asking the right questions; but if you don't ask the right questions, the exit interview is a lost opportunity. When employees are leaving, they have no reason to hold anything back. Many times they are willing to tell you a bunch of things they would normally not share with you because of the fear of losing their job. Now the double-edge sword, as you can expect, is that they may choose to condemn certain employees or supervisors they simply did not get along with, so you have to be smart about this interview.

Exit interviews also may give you a behind-the-scenes look at the operation from the perspective of an employee. You are not personally working all positions in the kitchen, so you cannot possibly see, experience, and feel every moment of every position in your kitchen. You may learn things about the position—e.g., that it is too much work, that the employees need to be challenged more, or maybe that there are problems with certain relationships. Whatever the case, if you ask enough questions, you are bound to learn something.

Next, you need to have a checklist for all the items the exiting employee may have that the property needs to retrieve. Manuals, uniforms, pagers, car stickers, security passes, keys, and so on. Every property is going to be a little different, but this list is important. If you are leasing your uniforms, there needs to be a system of canceling the set so you do not continue to pay for it.

Then there is the reconciling of paychecks, the current week's hours and vacation days. If you do not have an exit interview or termination form already available, you will want to create one so that the system is complete and consistent. Termination forms are also discussed in Chapter 15.

Never Forget Where You Came From

This is important for everyone in all professions. Chances are there is somebody somewhere who helped you get where you are today, whether a favorite teacher, coach, or relative. Somebody who made that light bulb go off in your head. These are very special people. Don't ever forget the special people who gave you the gift of inspiration. Be loyal to them. There are too many opportunists out there who would rather step on your back than help you. In my kitchen, what goes around, comes around. I've been saying it for years; you help me and I will help you, but first you have to help yourself. If someone helps you, be respectful and send them a thank you note.

> **"Never, never, never forget where you came from!"**

You have to understand something about the type of people who are always helping others. These teachers and mentors do not grow on trees. The art and responsibilities of mentoring can be sometimes hard to find in our fast-paced, Internet-flooded, I-want-to-jump-from-the-ground-onto-the-porch-without-taking-any-steps environment we live in today. There are people who live to teach and mentor. Their drive comes from watching people blossom through their nurturing care. To see one of their own go out into the world and be successful gives them great pride. They never ask for anything. They don't ask for money or recognition, nothing. Their thanks comes from the success of their pupils, whether they thank them or not.

Don't ever forget the people who have helped you. Send a card every now and then to thank them. Send them a card to tell them how you are doing, how your life and job are progressing. Or, better yet, call; they will be proud, they will be more thankful than you will ever know, and you will continue to inspire them to keep doing what they are best at—mentoring.

There are a handful of young people and professional chefs who call me on a regular basis. They want to catch up, tell me about their family and job. They share with me their latest challenges, and we talk through them. Many times they want to talk about the latest job offer they have received. I am always so proud to hear how respectful, responsible, and accomplished they are becoming. I am proud that they always want to do the right thing; that's why they call. They have a great set of values and a conscience. I always take time out for them, always.

Never, never, never forget where you came from!

Chapter 12

Incentive Programs

Incentive programs are a great, positive motivational resource that everyone should employ. Incentive programs can be whatever you want them to be. Some cost and others can be designed to need little monetary support. What you do need is management support. Without that, you are dead in the water. The secret with any plan is to design it first, put it on paper, and then propose it to the general manager. Don't go into the general manager's office with a half-baked idea without a plan. In this chapter, I discuss several programs I am currently using. They took many hours to develop, and you can adapt them to fit into your own program.

> **"Only those who dare to fail greatly can achieve greatly."**
>
> **—Robert F. Kennedy**

One important rule about incentive programs—they will only be successful if you nurture them, follow through with them, and be consistent and fair in them. They don't run by themselves; the momentum comes from the top—YOU! You decide if you want to lead, inspire, teach, motivate, reward, and give people a reason and an incentive to believe, to do better, to excel, and to be great. As a leader, you have that power.

Steward Program

I talk about Product Champions throughout this book. I am excited about this particular program, as it focuses on our stewarding program and the way in which we hire, train, and retain good people. I am sure we all share some frustration in this department, as normally it has the most turnover. Why? It is typically the least paid, trained, and educated position on-site. I have made it one of my missions to do something about it, starting with the

Steward Product Champion. That is why I started with this program and why I am most proud of it. You should want to do special things for the talented people in your department, but what are you going to do for this important group? I begin discussion of this program in Chapter 4.

The overall goal of the Stewarding Program is to educate, recognize, and reward stewards. We want them to know they are as special as the chefs, students, and cooks. Meetings are held with them to find out how we can make their job easier and to find out where they are having problems. It is vital to follow up with their recommendations and to fix items or machines they mention as not working properly. Many times these problematic items or machines will go unnoticed and not fixed for months, because we do not work the steward station. When you get things fixed quickly after they have been reported, your staff will appreciate you a whole lot more. It shows you care about them.

Second, I wanted to come up with a program that allowed stewards to *see* their own successes. They need to see the light at the end of the tunnel; the stewards need to know that if they work hard they can receive rewards and recognition. It has been a hugely successful program and has given stewards a sense of urgency and a desire to do great. As a result, we have been able to keep dishwashers longer.

Okay, so here is how I see it. You hire a dishwasher, tell them how important they are to your kitchen, point them to the dish machine, and say: "Welcome!" We have to do better than that. In my opinion, we have to paint a picture for all our employees; we have to lead them to the light at the end of the tunnel. Referring back to a part of our mission statement—a reason for being—we must show them our goals and show them how they can realize theirs. If all they see is a pile of dishes every night, exactly what can they possibly aspire to?

I think it is really important to know your employees. Where do they come from? Do they have family and kids? We need to paint the picture so they can see what happens if they work hard; they need to be able to see that if they are reliable and consistent in their work, they will be rewarded. I want to show them the year's calendar and give them personal goals to hit and how they will be rewarded when they do. I have started a few programs for the stewards on my team. Here are a few of my ideas:

- First, develop a *Steward Product Champion* program and encourage the stewards to seek other employees to sit on this committee. They will champion the concept and be in charge of holding a steward's meeting.

- Develop a *Calendar of Success.* Divide the year into quarters. Determine standards or goals for the stewarding staff to aspire to: for example,

be consistent and never late, always show up for shift, work hard, prepare clean records, be nonconfrontational. Come up with your set of
standards and review their progress every quarter. If they score high
in all categories, they will receive their incentive.

- Some incentives we have used include a fifty-cent per hour raise after
  their first quarter, *Gold Cards* (discussed below), three days off and forty
  hours of pay, gift certificates, $100 bonuses, a new pair of work shoes,
  dinner for two from our restaurant, and gift baskets around the holidays.

Yes, some of these incentives cost money. But you will save money in the
long run by rewarding them for being great employees. Set up your calendar
of success, propose it to your general manager, and put it into the budget.
Show the dishwashers when, how, and why they can get their rewards. Now
you have started a team! Someone figured out that firing and hiring a new
employee costs between $3,000 and $5,000 after all the training, paperwork,
and human resource work. So, you make the call, where do you want to
spend your time and money?

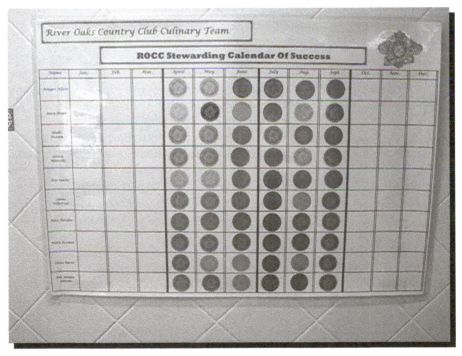

Prominently display the Steward Calendar of Success.

Gold Card Program

The *Gold Card* program was established to reward employees for excellence, for those who have gone above and beyond what is expected. An employee who collects three Gold Cards is eligible for a day off with pay or a complete dinner for four to take home and share with his or her family. Employees who have nominated successful candidates and employees who have received Gold Cards are recognized at the workout sessions.

There are three ways to receive a Gold Card:

1. Any member of the River Oaks Country Club (ROCC) Culinary Team can request an RREF (Recognition and Reward for Excellence Form) from my office. All forms have serial numbers and are signed out by the employee. The employee who fills out the form nominates a fellow colleague, making a case that the candidate is worthy of this distinction. All requests are evaluated every four weeks by the leadership team. The nominating party may be asked to attend this meeting to further validate the candidate.
2. Any employee who wins an MVC (Most Valuable Culinarian) Award (described later in the chapter) receives one Gold Card.
3. Any employee who comes up with an idea, policy, or procedure that is used by management that saves the club significant money or improves our work environment receives a Gold Card.

This program has worked very well in our kitchens. Currently, the culinary team is piloting it for the entire club with the hope that it will become a club-wide incentive. I love this program, because it involves everyone. Everyone can take part, be accountable, be *empowered,* and feel good about making a difference. Dishwashers, stewards, purchasing staff, chefs, students—anyone can recognize and reward excellence. Everyone can make a difference. It feels good to praise employees in a public way, to find someone doing something right, and it is great to regularly recognize employees for doing a fantastic job. Oftentimes, in many professions, recognition is not done nearly enough. The rush of doing business overrides how we treat the very employees who make the business successful to begin with.

Recognizing and rewarding excellence is the most common Gold Card given out, and a day off with pay is the most popular incentive. I really try to make a big deal out of the dinner for four for the employee to take home. Food makes people happy; food is a celebration. I ask the employees to give me notice when they want to take their dinner-to-go home so that I can be a part of the packing process. I want to be sure that we make it special. They get at least four courses, and we take good care of them. I want the employee to plan this special event, so that when they go home the family is expecting the special meal, and they can celebrate the recognition together. That is my goal. I want the employee to be proud of where they work, proud of the work they do, and proud of the beautiful meal they won and can share with their family.

As for the Gold Card given for an idea that saves the property money or employees' time, what better motivation to get everyone thinking on these topics. It is a way to tell the employees that you welcome and encourage their thoughts and ideas.

Green Beret Sous-Chef Program

We discussed the Green Beret program in detail in Chapter 11. What there is left to say here is that there is no better feeling than helping young professionals achieve greatness. The secret in this program is to manage it well. It is a bit of a chess match to maintain top sous-chef candidates, graduating some, enrolling new candidates, and not going over your labor budget. Chances are, once you have mentored a few good sous chefs, the word will get around that you can help employees reach their first executive chef jobs. Some take longer to master all the skills needed to be an executive chef, so there is no real timeline involved here. When someone is ready and you are willing to certify so, that is when it is time for the chef to go for his or her first big job.

I believe that the chefs you have who are interested in this program will continue to learn how to cook every day. They will focus on banquets, food preparations, and developing their recipe manuals and resources. If they don't, they are already missing the boat. In my kitchen, if you are not learning about cooking on a daily basis, there is a big problem. Chances are you are not paying attention to anything around you. I already expect talented people to be learning every day.

My job with the Green Beret candidates, I believe, is to empower them as much as possible. I work with them on scheduling, labor budgets, managing people, participation in member meetings, walking the dining rooms to check set-ups, food costs, and so forth. Basically, I help them on everything but cooking. As I have stated at several points throughout this book, I believe management skills are where our field is weakest. This is why the Green Beret program is important. When the time is near for a sous chef to move on, we even set up mock interviews for the sous-chef candidate. My general manager helps me with this. He puts the candidates through a hard interview, as the prospective general manager. I also set up a mock member interview as well. The more exposure, the better for the sous chef. The problem is, in many cases, executive chefs do not train in these departments. We need to do better to help mentor our chefs.

> **"I love young kitchens, because they are full of life and full of spirit."**

MVC Awards

The Most Valuable Culinarians (MVC) awards have been developed to recognize and reward excellence among ROCC culinary team members. Once a year, up to three employees can be recognized for their outstanding work. The recipients are nominated by their peers and receive a certificate, two Gold Cards, and a trophy. There are three MVC categories and their qualifications are below.

COMMITMENT TO EXCELLENCE AWARD

Given to the culinarian who displays the most overall day-to-day dedication to their profession and to the River Oaks Country Club's culinary team. This culinarian:

1. Follows, and instills in others, the guiding principles
2. Thinks ahead
3. Strives to always do his or her best and improve everything
4. Works efficiently and clean, never afraid to take on more responsibility
5. Is a team player
6. Displays a great concern for day-to-day operations of the club, in particular department as well as others
7. Always looks to see what else he or she can do
8. Does whatever it takes
9. Respects the knowledge and experience of supervisors as well as fellow employees
10. Always has a professional attitude and is crisp and clean

PROFESSIONALISM AWARD

Given to the culinarian who displays the most positive and consistent attitude of a Professional Chef. This culinarian:

1. Always has a positive attitude
2. Works and communicates well with his or her peers
3. Shows up on time and is concerned about day-to-day operations

4. Is able to execute tasks in a timely and efficient manner without sacrificing quality
5. Always strives to learn something new

CLEAN AND CRISP AWARD

Given to the culinarian who displays a consistent Clean and Crisp appearance every day. This culinarian:

1. Is always in a clean and complete uniform: necktie, apron, name tag, hat, and proper footwear
2. Is cleanly groomed and (for men) shaved
3. Works in a clean and organized manner and properly prepares mise-en-places
4. Consistently has a clean station and practices how to work clean every day

I think these are great categories in which to recognize chefs. The concepts of each are important in all professions, and they are self-explanatory. I love the clean and crisp award, because you have to practice to be clean. You can't just decide today that you are going to work clean; chefs have to work at it.

Distinguished Visiting Chef Program

We have developed a Distinguished Visiting Chef program wherein chefs and culinary teams are invited to stage demonstrations for our members and staff, prepare specialty wine dinners, and conduct practice sessions. These visits are very entertaining for our members and have proven to be invaluable learning tools for our staff. What better way to inspire your team than to bring an established chef in to showcase his or her talent. This is a great educational tool and benefits everyone.

To acknowledge these distinguished guests, we have a dedicated wall in our main kitchen for displaying pictures of these distinguished visiting chefs.

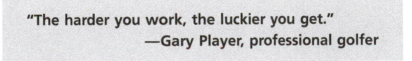

"The harder you work, the luckier you get."
—Gary Player, professional golfer

Again this program adds prestige to our kitchen. It keeps everyone on their toes, as we want to showcase our kitchen and our pride in it to chefs from all over the country. It also keeps our chefs from getting stagnant. They constantly have to be sharp, because someone is always touring our facility. We want to set the standard in our industry, so it is up to everyone to stay focused.

Top Gun Award

Top Gun candidates are nominated by their peers, and the top five candidates are selected by a committee. In accepting the nomination, they are asked to write a 300-word essay on why they should receive the award. The winner is awarded a trophy and a four-to-six-week externship at a prestigious property in the United States or abroad. Transportation and housing costs are provided by the club. Upon returning, the Top Gun employee is expected to give a presentation to the rest of the staff on the experience.

> **"There is no better feeling than helping someone!"**

We have sent chefs to Westchester Country Club in New York; The Sagamore Resort in New York; the Balsams Grand Resort Hotel in Dixville Notch, New Hampshire; Oak Hill Country Club in Rochester, New York; Bagatelle, a two-star restaurant in Oslo, Norway; properties in New Zealand; and many more places. This is a great opportunity for both the chef *and* the property, as the award winner learns a lot and brings back great ideas. It also gives all your chefs something to shoot for, a goal.

The bottom line for incentive programs is *do something!* Make a plan and feel good about the fact that you are helping young people grow, you are helping employees realize their goals. It is a special accomplishment, and it will certainly help you love your job even more. *There is no better feeling than helping someone!*

Chapter 13

Discipline and Competition

I have always believed that competition in anything is good. Whether it is in grade school, high school, or in life. Competition is good for your health. It keeps you focused and sharp, and it makes you study and work hard. Imagine for a second if we did not have any competition in life. We would all be fat and lazy. If there is no competition, you don't have to work hard at anything, just keep doing what you are doing. You are in no danger of losing. What is the point? We all would be in a galactic space of nothingness. If you keep doing what you have always done and no more, you will keep getting what you always get and nothing more or possibly something worse, because everyone will start passing you by. The best golfer in the world cannot stay number one forever. If he were to rest on being great, because he is great and he is number one, if he were to rest on his laurels and stop practicing he would soon no longer be number one.

> **"I play to win, I just love to win!"**
> **—Charles Carroll, 2005 Houston Texans' Tailgater**
> **of the Year**

Think about kids' sports. Now, I am not one of those crazed parents who gets in fights with the coaches, referees, or other parents, I just like to see the kids do their best and, most of all, start to learn discipline at a young age. When I was in sports, I was on time, in line, hard working, and all that. I worked hard on the drills to better my skills. That is all about discipline. It is also all the stuff we need to be a responsible adult. As adults, we have to have discipline in our lives and in our kitchens. Now, if a psychiatrist or other doctor, gets a hold of what I'm about to say, I am sure they would set me straight; but here it goes.

Put Forth Your Best Effort

Since when is it okay *not* to do your best? Since when do we not keep score? Since when is it okay not to be disciplined? Since when are you not supposed to encourage your child to score? I don't get it. Where did the discipline go? It is important to teach our kids at a young age that it is not okay if the ball goes past them because they made no effort to catch it. Kids need to be taught from a young age that success is as much in the effort, as it is in the accomplishment. When in life is losing really okay? *"Hey, George, you lost that account; but it is okay, we're not keeping score."* I know there is a fine line there; but I would like to see a little more discipline. It is okay to make a mistake; it is NOT okay not to give your best, not to give 100 percent. And guess what? People keep score in real life.

> **"It is okay to make a mistake; it is NOT okay not to give your best, not to give 100 percent. And guess what? People keep score in real life."**

My parents had a lot to do with my discipline and focus as an adult, and I'm so glad they did. Well, I am glad now, but when I was a kid, I wasn't so happy about it. When you are a kid, you do not think about discipline. I grew up in a country inn in Vermont. At the Rabbit Hill Inn, in the bolstering town of Waterford, there were eight days in the week. When growing up in a family business, you are it, you do everything from stocking the bars, cooking, prepping, snow shoveling, street sweeping after the winter season (that was my favorite, not!). If you grew up in the snow, you know all about the sand left on the roads in the spring. Well, my dad insisted that we sweep the half-mile street that went around the Inn. It would take a week for the three of us to do this. There are four kids in our family, and we all worked hard. But we were disciplined, and a switch doesn't flip that on. It has to be taught to you, instilled in you. You have to lead by example and also live it. Discipline is accountability, a great characteristic to have!

> **"If there is a way to do it better, find it."**
> **—Thomas Edison, inventor**

I believe there is a great separation among the generations. How did that happen? Where did it start? Why are the values of children different than those of our grandparents? Can we blame it on the computer age, the Internet, video games, or because both parents work? Is it because our world has become too focused on a I-need-it-right-now mentality that we lost our values along the way? My kids have so many more distractions than I did when we were kids. There were two TV channels when I grew up; my kids have 802 (yet many nights we can't find anything we want to watch). Yahoo, YouTube, MySpace, IM (Internet messaging), Web sites, text messages, cell phones, pagers at the age of 10—you name it, technology and its distractions are everywhere. I never had a cell phone until the age of 32. Try explaining that to your 12-year-old daughter.

There is a startling void in our leadership today. Dr. Rick Rigsby, who I mentioned before, author of *Lessons from a Third Grade Dropout* (Nashville, TN: Nelson Ignite, 2006), talks about this in his book. Executives, CEOs, the clergy, and coaches are being arrested for not being honest, not following the law, for covering up scandals, and for hiding money or debt. A favorite pastime for many is questioning the value of our political leaders. All of the mentoring figures we have looked up to in the past are now front-page news—but for negative reasons. Is our world moving so fast that we have to lie, cheat, or steal just to keep up? What can we do to change this?

When I was an apprentice, I would carve ice every chance I had so that I could become better at it. This took a lot of work, setting up an ice-carving station, collecting and arranging the tools, toting 300-pound blocks of ice around. I would carve four or five blocks a week. I did not get paid for it; I just *wanted* to do it! When I was working toward my first Culinary Olympic Team at the age of 23, it took several months of preparation. Many days and nights when other staff members were off enjoying the weather, I was sequestered inside, studying, and practicing to make the team. This was probably the most difficult and challenging time for me, because I wanted to be with my friends.

> **"I can't imagine any better high for a chef than to represent his country."**

My point is, do we see this style or effort today? It kills me when I ask a student or cook if they can stay a little longer because the VIP 10-course-meal prep is a little behind and the cook looks at me like I asked to pull every tooth out of his or her mouth with a pair of needle-nose pliers. The cook's pained look at the idea of staying longer than scheduled was tragic. Whereas, when I was a young professional, you would not be able to keep me away from such an event. My question would be: *"Can I come in on my own time, Chef?"* There is a major difference when you compare yesterday's workforce to today's.

I don't have all the answers, but I do know it all comes back to our surroundings. What is the atmosphere around your kids, around your employees, around your property? What is the discipline like? If the environment does not support positive discipline, the inhabitants will suffer. Try to accomplish anything of great value without personal discipline. Of all the kitchens you have seen, how many of them were sloppy, dirty, no real home for anything, confusing, and the equipment, carts, pots, pans, and boxes of nobody-knows-what stacked all in disarray? You have seen these kitchens. If an employee is in such a kitchen long enough, it becomes that person's standard of operation.

If the uniform policy is sloppy, if the executive chef does not present himself professionally, the staff will not either, simple as that. You need to set your standards in everything you do, and then live by them. This is how the guiding principles we have developed come into play. You have to live by them. All my professional life I have dressed classically as a chef with necktie and everything. It has been the only way for me to enter a kitchen. I have to keep after my staff, constantly reminding them to wear their culinary ties and to wear their name tags on the left breast of their jacket. What thrills me later is when I see them at their new property looking as professional as ever. This standard has stayed with them.

Lead by Example

Have you ever noticed the difference in work ethic between the employee who shows up for work five minutes before his shift and the employee who comes to work 45 minutes before his shift? Which one do you think is more disciplined, more ready for work, more prepared, more methodical about their day? I don't mean arriving so early one or two days a week; I mean showing up to work early as a habit. Have you ever heard the expression, "If you show up for work on time, you're late!"? There is a lot to be said about that. When I was at the Balsams Grand Resort, where most of the employees lived on the property, I strongly encouraged the employees to come in early enough to eat breakfast. This provided a healthy start to the day and gave them an opportunity to plan their day and get organized. The employees who did this on a regular basis were more attentive, sharper, and more disciplined. The employees who came rushing in with their tie and apron in their hand, punching in just in the nick of time would end up wasting 45 minutes of the day just getting acclimated.

I am telling you all this not just as an attempt to get you to go to work earlier but simply to encourage you to be disciplined and on time, to schedule and follow up. If you say you are going to do something do it. Show up early! That is the message. Show up and show up early. This is a special discipline that your entire staff will follow if you lead. If you make a habit to show up five minutes after the scheduled time, your staff will do the same. If you apply the "show up early" concept to your life, there is a certain amount of discipline that will follow, it just happens.

The way you lead and comport yourself reflects in the way others on your team present themselves.

Culinary Competitions

My life is full of competition, which I am very proud of. I have had seven affiliations with various Culinary Olympic teams. I am very proud of all the accomplishments of our teams. The American Culinary Federation (ACF) sponsors Culinary Olympic teams to compete in this international competition held every four years in Germany. I can't imagine any better high for a chef than to represent his or her country. Competing in these Olympic competitions has changed my life; it has driven me more than I could have ever imagined. It pushes me to be better every day. The research and sharing I do with other chefs and teams is priceless. You can't go to school or find a work experience that matches this experience. As I said before, it is not for everyone; but the chefs who compete learn a lot about life, teams, and spirit. They learn a lot about themselves and see parts of the world they might never have seen.

Chefs who choose to compete and *stick with it* usually are very driven, disciplined, and successful.

There is a contingent in the ACF who thinks money should not be spent
to send teams to the Olympics. I have to believe that 99.9 percent if not 100
percent of the people in opposition to the idea of spending money on this
have either never competed or never had an opportunity to be a part of a
team that represents the United States. It is okay not to compete, but do not
hold back the progress of those who wish to or those who benefit from the
research and development that the team competition returns to the cooks
in their kitchens. We have better chefs in the United States because of it.

Some people are against the competitions, but they sure don't mind
hiring the people who have competed. Many of the skills you admire in the
chef just hired were learned in the competition environment. You don't have
to compete, but at least respect the work and the thousands of hours of
commitment by chefs, properties, and families doing their best to support
the chefs' culinary arena.

Remember, competition is healthy. It provides a healthful environment.
In my kitchen, if you are a sous chef and you are not doing your job or
pushing the envelope, you are going to get steamrolled and someone will
rip that job from you.

Chapter 14

Did You Listen Well the First Time?

How many people think "good" is good enough? *That is pretty good. I like it. That is good. Good stuff. He is a good guy. I think it tastes good. Good idea. Good thinking.* When you read those sentences, how excited did you get? Are you inspired now? If you are okay with it and like how it sounds, I hope you have a good job, that your food is pretty good, and the atmosphere in your kitchen is good; that your employees have a good attitude; and that you have a good salary, too. If you are okay with good, you are all set—you are good.

How about these sentences: *That is awesome. I love it. That is fantastic. Great stuff. He is an all-world guy. That tastes unbelievable. Super idea. Brilliant thinking!* Which sentences do you want to be a part of—the good or the superlative sentences? Do you aspire to have people use those types of words about you, your work, and your food?

So, how are you *Finding Time to Be Great?* Let's review how you are going to set up your kitchen. The difference between good and great is attention to detail.

Self-Assessment

First, you need to do a self-assessment to be sure you are committed to being great. Be sure you are in the right frame of mind. Make sure you feel great about yourself and the potential of your kitchen. You have to live and breathe it. You want it to be great every day, because your staff is going to follow your lead. If you go into it halfway, it will only be that *good.* Discover a hobby— such as working out—that takes your mind off work for a short period and helps to refocus you on what is important.

Assess Your Current Team

Find out the talent and culinary level currently in your kitchen. How many culinarians do you employ now? *Make a promise to yourself only to hire culinarians.*

Build Your Leadership Team

The very first step in being successful is to surround yourself with great people. The leadership team will help you to develop all your programs and to set policies. Your team will be vested in the programs they helped develop, and their commitment will trickle down to the entire staff.

Support from Your General Manager

Although most of the programs I've outlined do not cost anything, it is vitally important to get support from your general manager. Please take the time to think your plan through thoroughly, outline all of your programs, and establish how you are going to implement them. Set up a meeting with your

Bring other members of the property leadership into your culinary team.

boss and present your plan. You cannot just read this book, pass your boss in the hallway, and say, "Hey, Boss, I wanted you to know I am going to start up some really cool programs. I am going to build the best team." That does not work. That is lip service. Be sure your word means something. If you say you are going to do something, make sure you do it. Put your plan on paper; discuss all your research; and explain how you are going to put the plan in place. Your manager will be impressed with your organization and will be more apt to support it. Many times, the chef's success is in direct proportion to the support he gets from the general manager. So, it is up to you to get the general manager vested into the program.

Mission Statement and Guiding Principles

The first step for your leadership team is to develop the culinary team's mission. You can't work together as a team, toward a common goal, if you don't have established and agreed-upon goals and a mission. It is as simple as that. Once the mission statement is finished, work on your guiding principles, the principles that your team will live by every day. These guiding principles will help your employees see the total picture. The guiding principles are the rules. You cannot play the game unless you know the rules.

Identifying Your Kitchen's Immediate Needs

Find out what areas your kitchen is weakest in and identify the problems. Develop Product Champions with your leadership team and work toward new programs to solve the kitchen challenges. The Product Champions program is a huge tool; I hope you take advantage of it. (See Chapter 4 to review development of Product Champion and Leadership Team programs.) Multiple brains working toward a common goal is infinitely better than one person trying to do everything on his or her own. You will accomplish so much more as a team than by trying to pound it out by yourself.

Create an Educational Environment and Incentive Programs

Constantly work toward creating a fantastic environment in your kitchen. Remember, if you build it, they will come. It is my opinion that an educational environment is the number one reason people will want to work for you. That is a pretty bold statement, don't you think? So, if you agree with me, this now becomes your top priority. It is not uncommon for young people to be a product of their environment. So what is your kitchen environment?

Fill your kitchen with several, great high-end oils and vinegars, not just one kind. The more flavors, the more creative and precise your chefs can be. Start making your own seasonal blends, toast some spice blends and rubs, and make this part of your kitchen recipe manual. The more seasonal blends, oils, vinegars, and wines your chefs have around them, the better chance they will take the time to season correctly and more efficiently. If you expect your chefs to taste everything, place containers of tasting spoons all around your kitchen, and they will taste! *Your kitchen is what you want it to be.* Your chefs will pick up habits and skills from their surroundings.

Program Survival

After going through all this work, you need to put programs in place and follow through on them to be sure they all survive. The mistake that most programs make is not incorporating any preventive maintenance programs. Use solid concepts to ensure your programs' survival. Make the first set of goals and objectives challenging but realistically achievable, then build on that success.

I can't emphasize enough the importance of coming up with a plan of action first, so you don't get frustrated. Develop your leadership team, mission statement, and guiding principles, and then quickly determine what immediate challenges are important for your kitchen. Identify and prioritize them. This now becomes the leadership team's first set of projects. Remember, your leadership team does not have to be made up of only kitchen staff. Invite other department heads who you think will be great contributors to the group. The perspective from someone outside of the kitchen is just as valuable.

How Long Is All This Going to Take?

It is worth the time and effort to put these programs into place. Hopefully these systems will forever after be a part of your routine kitchen procedures. Hopefully, you will never stop using any of these concepts. What will happen, which I encourage, is that the programs will constantly change—they need to change. To fit your organization, they constantly need to change. All of the ideas I have shared with you in this book may or may not fit exactly to your program. I hope that I have inspired you to take some of these programs and develop them for your program. Don't be satisfied with good. Make a difference with your talent. Be proud to give tours of your kitchen and to discuss the programs and your staff, and be proud of how you trained them. There is no better feeling than to get letters from past Green Berets, thanking you for everything that your program did for them, helping them to realize their goals (see Chapter 11 for more on the Green Beret Sous-Chef program). Getting such a letter and helping someone to succeed is pretty special.

> ## "Don't be lazy, don't be satisfied with good—make a difference with your talent."

So, for those of you who think you don't have time for these programs, let's take a look:

What?	When?	How Long?
Leadership meetings	Every two weeks	1–1½ hours
One-a-day meetings	Every day	5–7 minutes
Product Champions	They meet on their own and report back to you	
Workout Sessions	Every six weeks	45 minutes to 1 hour
Sit-downs	Meet with each employee at least once a year	20–30 minutes

In the grand scheme of things, it takes very little time out of your day. When you look at the times listed above, look at the hours you work in a week and relate the amount of time to the positive energy you get out of the program—it is a no-brainer. Always remember how your staff feels when they become part of your program. They are part of the planning process. You will start to see progress in your kitchen. That is the best part of the process, seeing the progress! Besides, all of these programs are forcing you to be more organized and better prepared. Ultimately, your kitchen is more professional and more efficient, and you are as well. Who doesn't want a more professional and educational environment?

One last thing. Most of us have a slow period in the year. You may want to take advantage of this time to do a lot of this planning. When I first started the program, the leadership team met every week, because I wanted results right then! I still want results right now, but we have a set schedule that seems to work with our team. It is important to develop a schedule that works for your team. It is also important that you stick to it, and *Follow Through!* If you decide to cancel a meeting here and there, they will not take you seriously, and your programs will never develop. Once the schedules are set, you stick to them like a mealtime, period! *SEF: Schedule It, Empower Your Employees, and Follow Up!*

Chapter 15

Forms to Help You

Forms are a way of life. But forms are only as good as the information you put on them and, more important, what you do with the information once you have filled them out. There are many forms that can help you with the programs we have talked about. To drive home your mission and your brand, I recommend that you put your logo on all of your forms. Your logo should mean something. If we put our logo on something, I tell my staff, we are guaranteeing that we have a great product. It has to be.

All the forms mentioned in this chapter can be found at the back of the book (see Certificates and Forms, page 140). If you would like electronic copies of these forms, please visit www.CulinaryLeadership.com where you can download customizable templates for your own use.

Culinary Certificate

We present all new employees with a certificate, printed on heavy, white stock paper with blue lettering and a red border that is suitable for framing. Designed easily on the computer, the document is a beautiful 8″ × 10″ certificate. On the bottom, left corner, there is a gold seal with a red, white, and blue ribbon attached. The certificate includes the date the employee became the newest member of the River Oaks Country Club (ROCC) Culinary Team, the mission statement, as well as the signatures of the general manager and myself.

Gold Card Award

The Gold Card Award is a gold, 6″ × 10″ certificate, printed in landscape format, and it includes the name of the employee, date of the recognition, and signatures of the general manager and myself. When an employee wins a gold card, we place a gold ROCC seal on the bottom, left corner. When the employee is recognized for a second gold card, we present another gold card with two seals on it and so on. When the employee receives three gold cards, he or she receives a day off with pay.

Guiding Principle Card

This is a great tool that makes it easy for employees to carry a copy of the guiding principles with them, at all times, and to refer to them as needed. We print them in both Spanish and English. This card is $2\frac{1}{2} \times 3$ inches and laminated. Again, this is one of our tools to help solidify and preserve our guiding principles.

Recognize and Reward Excellence Form

The RREF, or Recognize and Reward Excellence Form, is used by employees to nominate colleagues for a gold card. All employees are eligible for nomination; and any employee in the kitchens can nominate a fellow employee. It is an $8'' \times 10''$ form that lists our twenty guiding principles, with check boxes next to each of them. The nomination must be based on at least one of our guiding principles. There is a space to explain the reason for the nomination and an area for committee approval. A log of all nominations is kept in the executive chef's office.

Sanitation Inspection Form

These forms are very important to your program. You should create them in such a way that your employees can complete inspection of your kitchen efficiently and easily, without hindrance. I recommend that you go online and check out what your state recommends or requires in terms of food-service sanitation. They should have the complete inspection requirements available online. You can use basically the same kind of form.

Temperature Log

To log temperatures, we hang a clipboard by each cooler for which employees are responsible throughout the day. I don't need to tell you how important this is. The employee signs, dates, and makes note of the time of day when the temperature was taken. The state health inspector likes to see this form.

Stewards' Calendar of Success

This is one of my favorite tools. Devise a chart for your calendar year. Divide it into quarters and place all stewards' names on the form. You will devise your incentive rewards with your team. I gave you all kind of ideas in Chapter 12 that you can use here. Chart the progress of each of your stewards, and let them see how successful they are. I had gold, silver, and bronze seals made with our logo and The ROCC Culinary Team printed on them. We use these on this chart to symbolize success. You can laminate this form, post it in your kitchen, and refer to it during every stewards' meeting.

Stewarding Evaluation Form

Now that we have a Calendar of Success for the stewards, we need an evaluation form to accurately evaluate them on punctuality, attitude, efficiency, sanitation, appearance, and so on. After this is done, you then assign numeric scores to each category. Our scoring system is as follows:

85–100 is a gold medal.
75–84 is a silver medal.
65–74 is a bronze medal.

Any steward who averages gold for three months can win an incentive award. Remember, this calendar is posted in the kitchen for everyone to see.

Closing Procedures

How many times have you arrived at work to find that someone has left a piece of equipment on or that something was left unlocked? Pretty dangerous stuff. The larger the property, the more things you need to check. The closing procedures should include all equipment, doors, walk-ins—moving from one point in your kitchen clockwise, until all items are secure and turned off. Set up the form in the same order as your inventory is stored, so that the process moves along quickly. Your sous chef needs to date and sign the form each day at closing to indicate that the kitchen was closed properly.

Termination Form

Human resources departments are becoming more critical than ever. More and more documentation is needed for all hiring and firing of employees.

It is almost as bad as buying a house with all the papers you have to sign. Before you give the last check to an employee, it is good to have a checklist of all the items needed. The checklist should include keys of any kind, car decals, uniforms, pagers, radios, manuals, separation agreement, exit interview, and whatever else you can think of.

Burn-Out Sheet

We hang a clipboard by the purchasing office that lists all products that need to be moved out quickly. Obviously, we want to practice **FIFO** ("first in, first out"); but it is important to keep products moving so we have less spoilage. The purchasing agent or sous chef should walk through the coolers every morning and fill in the burn-out sheet with products that need to be moved. The rest of the staff is then able to work from the sheet during their preparations.

These are just a few ideas to aid you in your job. Try not to create paperwork for the sake of paperwork though. Forms are only as good as the information on them and what is done with the information once it is collected.

Chapter 16

Why Do It?

The quintessential question is: why do all this? What is the point? Well, I guess you don't have to. You can punch in and punch out, but as I have stated repeatedly, it won't get you very far. Don't ever get comfortable in your position, because that is when you start getting lazy. If you become complacent, you are done. You may as well punch out, because you are done. And while we are at it, let us not complain too much about our hours. Yes, we do have long hours; but so do a lot of other professions. Many of the programs I have outlined in this book don't take a lot of time once they are set up. What takes many hours is the development of the programs, and I'm giving you a big head start here. Besides, if you set the programs up, chances are you will end up saving time, because they compel your staff to communicate and successful communication is the secret to success.

I wish I had a dollar for every person I have toured through the kitchen and program. Many were very impressed. They say, "My, you've got a great job, great kitchen, your staff is so professional. It's nice to have a boss that works with you. I want your job, if you ever leave let me know." I would agree with them, I am fortunate. I do have a great job. In fact, I tell people it is the best chef's job in the United States. River Oaks Country Club is my White House. I would hope other chefs feel the same about their jobs.

> **"Instead of changing jobs, change the way you do your job!"**

I also remind people that this didn't happen overnight. I have worked hard all my life. Do you think for one second this kitchen was built using some cookie-cutter concept? Do you think for a second that the board, my boss, and the members would agree to build it if they did not have faith in my program and appreciate the job I have done in the past? Do you think someone just said, "Hey, Chef, we are going to build this kitchen because you are a nice guy?" Absolutely not. I worked hard all my life, and I am blessed with a great reputation. This came with a lot of teamwork, a lot of planning, a lot of history, and a lot of experience. It wasn't like this when I started. This incredible kitchen and program was not here before I started. If it were, they would not have had to hire a new chef.

It also kills me when others say, "Oh, I can't do that, I can't do this. My boss would never go for that." As a result, they do nothing. Build it, put it on paper, and make your case as to why it is the best thing to do for your property, guests, and employees, and you will be successful.

> **"The biggest mistake people make in life is not trying to make a living doing what they most enjoy."**
>
> **—Michael Forbes**

So why do it? Let's talk about being a pro chef, a professional. Are you a professional? What constitutes a professional chef? According to a dictionary, it is someone who is highly skilled and paid for what they do. I think there is a drastic difference between a professional athlete and a professional chef. If you are a pro athlete, chances are you can really play ball. If you are a paid cook or chef, it doesn't necessarily mean you can really cook or lead a team or even that you are professional, for that matter. In our field, the word pro applies differently. We have all met some outstanding chefs, great leaders, and team builders; these people are pros, real professionals. So, what do you want to be? Do you want to be a professional, a real pro, or do you want to be the water boy? Come on, step up, let's go. I'm giving you all the ideas I've been working on for twenty years. All of the models, concepts, and ideas in this book are real programs that work—they are right in front of you. I wish I had had this book twenty years ago. And if you find something like it for the culinary field, let me know so I can read it. Instead of changing jobs, change the way you do your job!

Get Started

So get going. Do something, be a professional, find time to be great. Schedule it, empower your employees, and follow up. My goal is to push you into being great, but the reality is that no one can push you as much as you can. It has to come from your heart first! Once you have it in your heart, then sometimes little pushes will help. I'll leave you with two stories, both of which I heard while I was working out.

I was talking to a nice guy I see from time to time at the gym. We call each other Chalupa, I'm not sure why but we do. He is a real nice guy, 32 years old, who loves his children and wife. He is a waiter for an Italian restaurant down the road. I asked him when he works, and he told me from 10:00 A.M. to 2:00 P.M. He said he didn't like working any more than that because it was too much work, and he gets tired. I was suddenly very sad for him. I was thinking, "What is wrong with you?" although I kept my thoughts to myself. I couldn't help but think he was wasting the healthiest time of his life. He told me his schedule, which ended every night with a six pack of Corona. He said his wife wasn't very happy with him, especially about the Corona every night. The point of this story is that you have to make hay when the sun shines. God gave you life, don't waste it. What is this guy going to do when he is 45 or 50 years old, with no real résumé or skills? How is he going to find a decent job that will pay him well enough to put his kids through school? What is he going to do then?

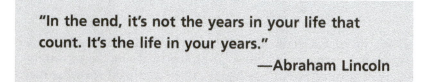

> **"In the end, it's not the years in your life that count. It's the life in your years."**
>
> **—Abraham Lincoln**

In another case, I was changing in the locker room and saw a guy I also see from time to time. "George" has two artificial legs that he slips on over his knees. Every time I see him I think, "God bless the guy." He is a regular at the gym, and nothing seems to stop him from doing anything. He is always in a good mood; in fact, some days he spends more time visiting than working out. It seems like he knows everyone.

Anyway, one day he took his legs off so that he could change over from shoes to sneakers, and then he slipped the legs back on. One of his friends stopped to talk. He started to ask him about his workout, how he could get on with the artificial legs, what kind of workout can he do, and does he ever get down about it. I was thinking, "Back off a little." But George smiled and said, "Man, I am so lucky. There are so many things I can do!" I was blown away! I got goose bumps. I was a little tired, but after hearing that story, I ended up beating myself to a pulp during that workout. How special is George's outlook on life? George inspired me that day.

Passion

Well, folks, we have gone over a lot of material here. As you probably can tell, this is my life, has been my life, and will be my life for many more years. This is what keeps me driving toward success. I am so fortunate that every day I still want more. The depressing thing can be, when you stop wanting more. When you *start* getting too comfortable in your position is when you *stop* pushing for success. This is a scary thing to think about, because often-times we get too complacent. Please be careful you never find yourself get-ting lazy or comfortable. This is why I count my blessings every day, because I still have so many goals I want to reach with my team. When you find yourself just "punching in and punching out," stop and give yourself a true evaluation, because this is truly the worst feeling in a job. And worse still, your staff will follow suit.

Cooking Provides Happiness

How often do chefs have an opportunity to make people happy? Every time we feed people is what I'm thinking. There are many times I come home at night and tell my wife, "We made a lot of people happy tonight." When I have that feeling, it makes my whole day. The art of food and the celebration of food at weddings, birthdays, holidays, and even funerals—food and our passion plays a very special role in everyone's life. Does a plumber make people happy, stimulate the customer's sensations? Does an electrician,

Incorporate your passion for creating wonderful food into all aspects of your professional life.

builder, engineer, or doctor? All are admirable professions, but my point is that we chefs make people happy with our craft. Have you ever been invited over to a plumber's house to work on pipes some Sunday afternoon, to an electrician's house to play around with a new fan? Not likely. But as chefs, we are constantly having friends over to share our craft, to cook with and for, and to enjoy a wonderful meal, making people happy. We are so fortunate that our profession makes people happy.

One More Thing

I have spent my time, throughout this book, trying my best to inspire you to be great, trying to show you how to find time to be great. Now I want to remind you not to forget to find time for your family, your friends, your neighbors, and your colleagues. I recently had my neighbors over for dinner: some steak, Alaskan King Crab, roasted potatoes with truffle oil, sautéed onions, sugar snap peas, and bok choy. The kids jumped in the pool, and we drank some wine, played music, and finished with some great cigars. My original plan was to work on this book all night, as I have very little quiet time to write. We ended up having the cookout at the last minute, and I am glad we did. Special times with special friends are priceless and don't happen enough. You have to "schedule it" but also allow for some flexibility and spontaneity. I am thinking that chefs are probably on the top of the list when it comes to bad scheduling: missed proms, rehearsals, dances, gymnastic shows, music recitals, ball games, birthdays. You name it, we have missed them all at one time or another. You have to *find time to be great* with your own family as well. I am writing to you from experience and not as an expert. In my opinion, we all probably need help here.

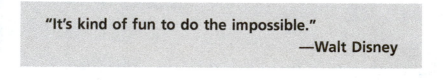

"It's kind of fun to do the impossible."

—Walt Disney

While I was writing this book, my dad was in the hospital. He is only 71 years old, but he had a rough eight months in the hospital. My dad loves to play golf. We hold an annual family golf tournament that includes an amazing group of friends that my brother and I consider family. Unfortunately, my dad was unable to attend the latest tournament. This is such a special time for us, as it is about great friends, great wine, supposedly some golf in there somewhere, and, of course, food. Every year I stock a couple coolers with food enough to make three-course meals for three nights to feed twenty guys. It is a lot of work, but the food is a special part of the weekend. Of course, everyone always ends up congregating in the kitchen. For my next house, I am going to build the kitchen first and then surround it with the rest of the house. Everyone wants to see you work with the food. That ideal kitchen will have living room-like amenities, with televisions, a stereo, bar stools, a high counter, and with a view of the entire house.

At our golf tournament, everyone congregates in the kitchen, peeling this, chopping that, and telling lies about how well they played golf that day. I would do anything to play one more round of golf with dad. Just one more round would be great. I would not want the round to end. At this point, I am hoping he gets a chance to read this book. My dad was a chef and my brother Greg is a chef. Obviously, Dad had a big influence on us. There is a saying, "Live Like You're Dying." I wonder how many of us take life for granted. Be sure you don't live life like Chalupa, where one day you wake up and ask yourself, "What have I done? How could I have let life pass me by?" I wonder how we all would look at life if we had a near-death experience. My recommendation would be not to wait for the near-death thing and make good now!

Final Thoughts

In closing, I hope I have inspired you. I never said being great was going to be easy. It is not what I've taught you but what you have learned that is important. I hope this book has helped you build your team, inspired you to function at a higher level and focus on the positive. Don't go through life with regrets. You can wish and dream forward, but you can't dream back. Don't ever regret, start today, do something extraordinary, and stop being ordinary. Be a Professional Chef, a real pro. And recognize that you have the power to make a difference in someone's life. How special is that!

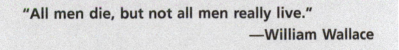

"All men die, but not all men really live."
—William Wallace

The first day of the rest of your life starts today!

Appendix A

Certificates and Forms

River Oaks Country Club

Recognizes

[Insert New Employee Name Here]

As a member of the ROCC Culinary Team

On this the 15ᵗʰ day of July 2007

THE ROCC CULINARY TEAM MISSION STATEMENT

To be recognized as the premier private country club Culinary Team in the United States
by sourcing and purchasing the highest quality product, enabling us to provide
our membership with the finest dining experience in the country.

To create a working atmosphere, according to our guiding principles,
where the highest standards of excellence, professionalism, leadership, respect,
and culinary pride are instilled in the Culinary Team. With an end result of growing culinarians
who not only reach their individual goals but grow into positions of culinary influence and leadership.

_____

General Manager C. J. Bendy, Jr. CCM

_____

Executive Chef Charles Carroll, CEC / AAC

Form 1 Culinary Certificate

Gold Card To Recognize and Reward Excellence

Awarded to

_____

On This 15th day of July 2007

A member of the River Oaks Country Club Culinary Team in recognition of their dedication and hard work.

_____
C.J. Bendy, Jr. CCM
General Manager

_____
Chef Charles Carroll, CEC / AAC
Executive Chef

Form 2 Gold Card Award

ROCC CULINARY TEAM GUIDING PRINCIPLES

1	Improve everything we touch.
2	Taste everything.
3	We are ladies and gentlemen serving ladies and gentlemen.
4	Commitment to excellence.
5	Treat our members and each other with respect and dignity.
6	Create a positive and safe work environment.
7	Use the proper tool for the proper job.
8	Be accountable.
9	Serve hot food hot and cold food cold; never serve an inferior product.
10	Uncompromising levels of cleanliness and sanitation.

11	Take pride in the chef uniform; be clean and crisp.
12	Ultimate kitchen and mental "mise-en-place."
13	Never lose a member.
14	Meticulously attend to every detail.
15	Be an ambassador of the ROCC Culinary Team.
16	Recognize and reward excellence.
17	Educate and motivate.
18	Consider "What are our options?"
19	Always ask "What can I do to help?"
20	Function as a team.

This is a copy of River Oaks Guiding Principle card. The principles are printed on 2½ × 3¼ cards and laminated. The card fits in the employee's wallet or breast pocket. You can buy the perfect size for your principles. Chances are your human resources department already has a machine to make laminated ID cards.

Form 3 Guiding Principle Card

RECOGNIZE AND REWARD EXCELLENCE FORM (RREF)

Instructions

This form is used to nominate employees to receive a Gold Card. Complete the necessary information below. Give specific reasons why you feel the person deserves this distinction. Return the completed form to Chef Carroll's office. Once evaluated, you will be informed of the decision.

Candidate Info

Name _____ ID _____

Reason(s) _____

_____

_____

_____

_____

_____

_____

_____

_____

_____

Nominated by _____ ID _____

Office Use

Received by _____ Date _____

Evaluated by _____ Date _____

Form 4 Recognize and Reward Excellence Form

ROCC SANITATION INSPECTION

Dry food storage

1.____ All food packages are closed.

2.____ All food storage and handling areas are free from evidence of rodent or insect infestation.

3.____ Dry bulk food items, such as flour, beans, sugar, etc., are stored in clean, labeled containers.

4.____ Food is not stored under unprotected or exposed water or sewer lines.

5.____ Food is stored off the floor to permit cleaning.

6.____ Food storage shelves, containers, and the area are clean and free from trash and empty boxes.

7.____ Foods are dated and/or placed on shelves in a manner that ensures *first in, first out*.

8.____ Home-canned or prepared foods are not used.

9.____ No dented cans are being held for use.

10.____ All food carts and speed carts are cleaned and sanitized before every use.

11.____ Toxic materials and pesticides are not stored with food items.

NOTES:

_____

_____

_____

_____

Form 5 Sanitation Inspection Form

Nonfood and chemical storage

1.____ Mops and cleaning equipment are not left standing in dirty water or area.

2.____ The storage area is clean and free from trash and food residue.

3.____ Toxic materials are labeled.

Refrigerators and freezers

1.____ All refrigerated cooked foods that are to be cooked are placed in shallow containers.

2.____ Foods are not stored together so air can circulate freely.

3.____ Freezers are clean and held at 0°F or lower.

4.____ Frozen foods do not show evidence of freezer burn or spoilage.

5.____ Frozen foods not in their original containers are wrapped or packaged, labeled and dated.

6.____ Raw meat items and eggs are not stored or thawing above cooked foods

7.____ Raw or thawing meat items are not stored above produce or eggs.

8.____ Refrigerated food items not in their original containers are well wrapped or packaged, labeled and dated. (Leftovers may be held no more than seven days before serving. Foods held at 45°F have four days holding time.)

9.____ Refrigerators are clean and the temperature is 41°F or lower.

NOTES:

_____
_____
_____
_____

Form 5 (*Continued*)

Food production and preparation area

1._____ All food-service equipment, appliances, walls, vents, and screens are clean.

2._____ All foods are cooked to proper internal temperatures (per local ordinance).

3._____ All food-service employees in the kitchen are wearing hair chef hats to cover hair.

4._____ All lighting is protected by shatterproof covers or bulbs.

5._____ Bottoms of pots and pans are free of dirt and grease.

6._____ Cutting boards are washed and sanitized between uses and when going between raw and cooked foods.

7._____ Employees do not smoke or eat in the food-preparation area. Drinking cups or glasses must be covered and contain a type of drinking straw device and NOT kept above work stations.

8._____ Employees infected with a disease or symptoms that can be transmitted by food are either sent home or restricted to non-food-contact activities.

9._____ Food-preparation equipment, such as grinders, choppers, mixers, knives, can openers, and all food contact parts are cleaned and sanitized between uses.

10.____ Food-service staff wash their hands thoroughly after coughing, sneezing, or any other form of contamination.

11.____ Food-service workers do not touch cooked food with their bare hands.

12.____ Frozen food is thawed properly.

NOTES:

_____
_____
_____
_____

Form 5 (*Continued*)

13.____ Potentially hazardous foods are held at the correct temperature. Hot foods are to be above 140°F, cold foods are to be below 41°F, and frozen food must be at 0°F at all times.

14.____ Steam tables or food warmers are not used to reheat or prepare food. Food temperatures are checked and monitored regularly with a clean and sanitized thermometer.

15.____ There is an accessible hand-washing sink in the kitchen. The sink area is clean, and it has soap and disposable towels.

16.____ Vegetables and fruits are properly washed before preparation.

Dishwashing area

1.____ A high-temperature dishwashing machine reaches a wash-cycle temperature of 140°F and a rinse-cycle temperature of 160°F (or temperatures listed in manufacturer's specifications).

2.____ A manual wash, three-compartment sink must contain either bleach sanitizing solution or iodine, verified using chemical strips.

3.____ Dishes, glasses, etc., are not stacked while wet.

4.____ If a low-temperature dishwashing machine is used with a chemical agent, the temperature and the chemical concentration must be up to the manufacturer's specifications.

5.____ No cracked or chipped dishes or glasses are present.

6.____ There is no evidence of food residue on "clean" dishes, pots, and pans.

7.____ Floors are kept dry and clean as much as possible.

NOTES:

_____
_____
_____
_____

Form 5 (*Continued*)

Food transportation

1._____ Food carts are clean and sanitized prior to use.

2._____ Meat and fish in transport are topped with bags of ice and are kept at 41°F or below.

3._____ Trays served to customers are brought back and washed thoroughly before reuse.

Garbage and refuse area

1._____ Garbage and refuse containers are in good condition with no leaks and kept clean. Washed and sanitized on a daily basis.

2._____ Garbage container (including outside dumpster) is kept securely covered.

3._____Loading dock is kept clean; barrels are neat and organized.

4._____All bread racks are stacked and picked up regularly by purveyors.

NOTES:

_____

_____

_____

_____

MAINTENANCE ISSUES:

_____

_____

_____

_____

_____

_____

_____

_____

Inspector's Signature: _____Date:_____

Department Head's Signature: _____Date:_____

Form 5 (*Continued*)

WEEKLY WALK-IN TEMPERATURE LOG

WEEK OF:_____

Walk-ins	DATE:	TEMP.	INITIAL:	TIME:
Banquet				
Garde-manger				
Freezer				

Walk-ins	DATE:	TEMP.	INITIAL:	TIME:
Banquet				
Garde-manger				
Freezer				

Walk-ins	DATE:	TEMP.	INITIAL:	TIME:
Banquet				
Garde-manger				
Freezer				

Walk-ins	DATE:	TEMP.	INITIAL:	TIME:
Banquet				
Garde-manger				
Freezer				

Walk-ins	DATE:	TEMP.	INITIAL:	TIME:
Banquet				
Garde-manger				
Freezer				

Walk-ins	DATE:	TEMP.	INITIAL:	TIME:
Banquet				
Garde-manger				
Freezer				

Walk-ins	DATE:	TEMP.	INITIAL:	TIME:
Banquet				
Garde-manger				
Freezer				

Form 6 Temperature Log

River Oaks Country Club Culinary Team

ROCC Stewarding Calendar Of Success

Name	Jan.	Feb.	Mar.	April	May	June	July	Aug.	Sept.	Oct.	Nov.	Dec.
Milagro Alfaro												
Stacy Boyer												
Gladis DeLeon												
Leticia Mancilla												
Jose Suarez												
James Villarreal												
Juan Morales												
Doris Escobar												
Eliseo Deras												
San Juana Galvan												

Form 7 Stewards' Calendar of Success

ROCC Stewarding Evaluation Form

ROCC STEWARD:_____DATE: _____ EVALUATION CHEF: _____

		MAX SCORE	TOTAL SCORE
I.	**PUNCTUALITY FOR SHIFT**		
	Unacceptable to be repeatedly absent	15	
	If late more than 15 minutes, need to call ahead of time	15	
II.	**ATTITUDE**		
	Positive	5	
	Friendly and cheerful	5	
	Respectful	5	
	Responds constructively	10	
	Gives good feedback	5	
III.	**EFFICIENT WORKER**		
	Takes initiative	10	
	Completes tasks given to him or her	10	
	Able to find projects on own; continues to find work when all tasks are completed	10	
IV.	**UNCOMPROMISING LEVELS OF CLEANLINESS AND SANITATION**		
	Always keeps sinks filled with clean soap water and sanitation water.	10	
	Never puts away unclean pots, pans, or china	10	
	Works in an organized manner	10	
V.	**APPEARANCE**		
	Wears proper and clean uniform	30	
VI.	**GOES ABOVE AND BEYOND**		
	Above: Excels in qualities defined in efficient worker	15	
	Beyond: Taking on additional duties and volunteering to participate and help beyond required duties	15	
VII.	**COMMUNICATION**		
	Communicates well with others	30	
VIII.	**FOLLOWS INSTRUCTIONS FROM SUPERVISOR AND CHEFS**		
	Responds within a reasonable amount of time	15	
	Always keeps a positive attitude when asked to do a job	15	
IX.	**TEAMWORK**		
	Functions as a TEAM	30	
X.	**ABLE TO ACCEPT CONSTRUCTIVE CRITICISM**		
	Takes direction well	15	
	Sees criticism as an opportunity to improve self	15	

Form 8 Stewarding Evaluation Form

Main Kitchen P.M. Closing Procedures

"Be Accountable, Ultimate Kitchen, Mise-en-place, Cleanliness and Sanitation, Attend to Every Detail"

_____Label and store all "overproduction" mise-en-place on Collins Room shelf.

_____Straighten walk-ins and freezers, label and date all parties on speed carts.

_____All spices and commentaries are neat and organized.

_____Last supervisor to check with stewards before he or she leaves.

_____Communicate with A.M. shift, about "pop-ups" or major changes on the dry-erase board.

_____All excess warmers emptied and returned to proper areas.

_____All sinks and counters are wiped clean and sanitized.

_____Check coolers and dry storage in storeroom to make sure all are locked.

_____Turn off:

    _____All Ranges   _____Flat Tops

    _____Convection and Combination Ovens   _____Toaster

    _____Char Grill   _____Conventional Ovens

    _____Wok   _____Heat Lamps

    _____Plating Table and Cabinets   _____Hot Boxes

    _____Four Kettles, unless stocks are working

    _____Two Swiss Braisers

Comments:_____

_____

_____

Signature of Closing Chef:_____ Date:_____

Form 9 Closing Procedures

RIVER OAKS COUNTRY CLUB
SEPARATION RECORD

Employee Name_____ Social Security No. _____

Department_____ Job title_____ _____Part time _____Full time _____On call

Employee Number_____ Date of Separation_____ _____ Seasonal _____ Temporary

Resignation:
❑ With notice   Days advance notice given_____
❑ Without notice

Is this person eligible for Rehire?   YES   or   NO

Reason:
❑ School
❑ Temporary/Seasonal Employee
❑ Health Reasons
❑ Military Service
❑ Personal Reasons
❑ Job Opportunity
❑ Relocation
❑ Resignation at Club's Request

❑ Better Benefits
❑ Transportation Problems
❑ Did not like type of work
❑ Walked off the job
❑ Never returned from leave of absence
❑ Retired
❑ No reason given
❑ Other (explain below)

Involuntary Separation:
❑ Unsatisfactory Work Performance
❑ Attendance or Tardiness
❑ Absent without calling a department manager
❑ Bank irregularity
❑ Theft or Dishonesty
❑ Drug or Alcohol related
❑ Time Clock Violation
❑ Insubordination
❑ Layoff
❑ Gambling on club property
❑ Unauthorized entry to Club property
❑ Unauthorized possession of club records

❑ Waste of material, destruction, or abuse of Club property
❑ Possession of Firearms
❑ Rudeness to a Member
❑ Fighting, threatening, or intimidating a Member or Employee
❑ Failure to follow instructions
❑ Failure to follow Safety Procedures
❑ Immoral Conduct
❑ Violation of Club Policy
❑ Falsifying Club Records
❑ Deceased
❑ Other (explain below)

Explanation of Circumstances
_____
_____
_____

I have read this "Separation Record" and understand it.

_____
Employee Signature   Date

_____
Supervisor Signature   Date

_____
General Manager   Date

INITIALS & DATE

HR_____

Payroll_____

Benefits_____

Verified by_____

(Please attach any documentation to this separation record.)

Form 10 Termination Form

Burn-Out Sheet: *Proteins*

Item:	Date:	Amount:

Form 11 Burn-Out Sheet

Burn-Out Sheet: *Produce*

Item:	Date:	Amount:

Form 11 (*Continued*)

Appendix B

Life and Work Tips from Chef Carroll

- Make a difference in someone's life.
- Constantly ask your staff their opinion.
- When traveling, carry thank you cards. Many times during your travels you meet people who have taken care of you or have hosted you in some way. No better time to write thank-you cards than on the plane home.
- Constantly ask yourself questions until you get all the right answers.
- Schedule time with your family...and follow through with your schedule.
- The most important thing in your life is your family; second is your job. You can't support your family without a job. Balance is important.
- Think big! Always think big.
- Never eat in an airport. Many times the temptation is to eat when you are waiting to catch a flight. Eat a solid meal before you leave the house, and if you do eat at airports, stay away from fried foods.
- Read! It's good for you. Read.
- Read what your boss reads.
- Focus to improve everything you touch.
- Never, never, never forget where you came from. Be sure to always honor and respect the people who have helped you throughout your career.
- Integrity is the consistency of what you say and what you do.
- Who do you admire the most? Practice to be like them.
- Always take advantage of your time while flying. I get so much work done on planes. No distractions, no phones, no business questions. Taking advantage of your time does not necessarily mean "working," although it is a good time to work. It could mean simply reading a

good book, writing special notes of encouragement to your staff, writing thank you cards, or if traveling with your family—spending quality time with your loved ones.

- Be a good listener. Most times it is best just to listen to what *everyone* has to say before making an assessment or responding.
- Start thinking about your workday the minute you get out of bed. Line your day up during your drive in to work. If you are like me, you need to carry a tape recorder in the car to record your ideas.
- Choosing to be kind will force your attitude to change.
- Commit to only hiring culinarians.
- Exercise!
- Call a family member at least once a week.
- Make mentoring a part of your legacy.
- What comes around, goes around.
- Your word should mean something.
- Show up early!
- Make an impact with your life and your work ethic.
- Always push to reach the top.
- If you think you're at the top, remember there is always more room at the top.

Appendix C

A Collection of Quotations

I am always asked if I have a collection of the quotations called out in each chapter. So for your reading pleasure, they are all compiled here.

"I knew someone had to take the first step, and I made up my mind not to move."
—Rosa Parks
Page: x

"Talent is cheaper than table salt. What separates the talented individuals from the successful one is a lot of hard work."
—Stephen King
Page: xii

"What most inspires me is working with young professionals and building great teams."
Page: 1

"One of the marks of true greatness is the ability to develop greatness in others."
—J. C. McCauley
Page: 3

"The beauty about my passion is that to this day, I have not stopped working to improve my qualifications."
Page: 3

"People don't care how much you know, until they know how much you care."
—John C. Maxwell
Page: 4

"Focus on your work, not the titles. If you produce beyond
expectations, the titles will come."
Page: 5

"YOU have the power to make a difference in the lives of
everyone you touch. That is pretty special."
Page: 7

"If you are not a team, you're just a crowd of people
standing in an empty room."
Page: 9

"To do a common thing, uncommonly well,
brings success."
—Henry Heinz
Page: 10

"The first rule of holes: When you're in one,
stop digging."
—Molly Ivins, columnist
Page: 11

"Success seems to be connected with action. Successful
people keep moving. They make mistakes, but they
don't quit."
—Conrad Hilton, hotel executive
Page: 12

"The more passionate the cook, the better the flavors."
Page: 15

"We are ladies and gentlemen serving ladies and
gentlemen."
—Herman Rusch
Page: 19

"We are what we repeatedly do. Excellence, then, is not an
act but a habit."
—Aristotle
Page: 19

"You may have stopped the bleeding but you have not
cured the patient."
Page: 21

"The most important single ingredient in the formula of
success is knowing how to get along with people."
—Theodore Roosevelt
Page: 22

"What people say, what people do, and what they say they
do are entirely different things."
—Margaret Mead, anthropologist
Page: 25

"If you want to be successful, put your effort into
controlling the sail, not the wind."
Page: 27

"SEF: Schedule, Empower, and Follow Up!"
Page: 28

"Do something about it! Stop complaining and do
something about it!"
—Torill Carroll
Page: 32

"Most importantly, think about this, people who feel good
about themselves produce good results!"
Page: 33

"A little nonsense now and then is relished by the
wisest men."
—Willy Wonka
Page: 33

"The awesome thing about a team is that it can
accomplish so much more than any one individual can,
and at a higher quality level as well."
Page: 35

"A good leader encourages followers to tell him what he
needs to know, not what he wants to hear."
—John C. Maxwell
Page: 36

"Leadership is calculated risk-taking."
—Ted Ward
Page: 40

"The measure of success is not whether you have a tough
problem to deal with but whether it is the same problem
you had last year."
—John Foster Dulles, former U.S. Secretary of State
Page: 41

"I not only use all the brains that I have, but all that
I can borrow."
—Woodrow Wilson
Page: 44

"They are vested in the program!"
Page: 45

"The only people who don't make mistakes are the people
who don't do anything."
—Phil Learned, CEC, AAC
Page: 46

"I won't live long enough to learn from my mistakes so I
have to learn from the mistakes of others."
—Joe Bendy
Page: 47

"Great leaders are never satisfied with current levels of
performance. They are relentlessly driven by possibilities
and potential achievements."
—Donna Harrison
Page: 47

"Communicate, communicate, communicate—until you
are sick of hearing yourself. Then communicate
some more."
—Jack Welch, former CEO of General Electric
Page: 48

"There is nothing more annoying than a weak
follow-through."
Page: 50

"If you don't have goals you are just punching in and out,
working aimlessly day after day."
Page: 53

"You need a mission for your staff, an overall objective,
and a clear sense of where your team is going."
Page: 54

"Your leadership team has to develop guiding principles,
goals, and mission statements that fit your organization
and your program."
Page: 56

"They will grow into positions of influence
and leadership."
Page: 57

"A successful man is one who can lay a firm foundation
with the bricks others have thrown at him."
—David Brinkley, television journalist
Page: 60

"You've got to love your people more than your position."
—John C. Maxwell
Page: 61

"He who has done his best for his own time has lived for
all times."
—Friedrich von Schiller, playwright
Page: 65

"Success is never final, failure is never fatal, it is courage
that counts."
—Winston Churchill
Page: 67

"You only get out of it, what you put into it!"
—Joe Bendy
Page: 70

"Genius? Nothing! Sticking to it is the genius! I've failed
my way to success."
—Thomas Edison, inventor
Page: 71

"No man will make a great leader who wants to do it all
himself or get all the credit for doing it."
—Andrew Carnegie, industrialist
Page: 73

"Anyone who influences others is a leader."
—Chuck Swindoll
Page: 75

"Do not confuse motion and progress. A rocking horse
keeps moving but does not make any progress."
—Alfred Montapert
Page: 77

"I just want to make it better! It is that simple."
Page: 81

"Improve everything we touch."
Page: 82

"Ask yourself the question, 'What if...?'"
Page: 82

"Complete every job asked of you better than it was
expected."
Page: 84

"You don't have to be great to get started, but you do have
to get started to be great."
Page: 84

"No person was ever honored for what he received. Honor
has been the reward for what he gave."
—Calvin Coolidge
Page: 85

"You miss 100 percent of the shots you never take."
—Wayne Gretzky
Page: 86

"If no one ever took risks, Michelangelo would have
painted the Sistine floor."
—Neil Simon, playwright
Page: 87

"There is no substitute for experience."
Page: 90

"Invest in your own future!"
"Don't cheat yourself!"
Page: 92

"You work like you feel."
—John Carroll
Page: 98

"I have made a pledge to myself that we are only going to
hire culinarians."
Page: 101

"You've got to have great athletes to win, I don't care who
the coach is. You can't win without good athletes, but you
can lose with them. This is where coaching makes
the difference."
—Lou Holtz, football coach
Page: 103

"Throw your heart over the bar, and your body
will follow."
—Advice from a veteran trapeze artist
Page: 107

"Never, never, never forget where you came from!"
Page: 110

"Only those who dare to fail greatly can achieve greatly."
—Robert F. Kennedy
Page: 111

"I love young kitchens, because they are full of life
and full of spirit."
Page: 116

"The harder you work, the luckier you get."
—Gary Player, professional golfer
Page: 117

"There is no better feeling than helping someone!"
Page: 118

"I play to win, I just love to win!"
—Charles Carroll, 2005 Houston Texans'
Tailgater of the Year
Page: 119

"It is okay to make a mistake; it is NOT okay not to give
your best, not to give 100 percent. And guess what? People
keep score in real life."
Page: 120

"If there is a way to do it better, find it."
—Thomas Edison, inventor
Page: 120

"I can't imagine any better high for a chef than to
represent his country."
Page: 121

"Don't be lazy, don't be satisfied with good—make a
difference with your talent."
Page: 129

"Instead of changing jobs, change the way you do
your job!"
Page: 134

"The biggest mistake people make in life is not trying to
make a living doing what they most enjoy."
—Michael Forbes
Page: 135

"In the end, it's not the years in your life that count. It's
the life in your years."
—Abraham Lincoln
Page: 136

"It's kind of fun to do the impossible."
—Walt Disney
Page: 138

"All men die, but not all men really live."
—William Wallace
Page: 139

Glossary

Accountability Being called to account for one's actions; answerable.

American Culinary Federation (ACF) The American Culinary Federation, Inc., is the premier professional chefs' organization in the United States, with more than 240 chapters nationwide and 18,000 members.

Apprenticeship One bound by legal agreement to work for another for a specific amount of time in return for instruction in a trade, art, or business.

Body Language The gestures, poses, movements, and expressions that a person uses to communicate nonverbally.

Brigade System The kitchen organization system instituted by Auguste Éscoffier. Each position has a station and well-defined responsibilities.

Burn-out Sheet A sheet filled out by a sous chef that includes the products that need to be used up before they spoil.

Calendar of Success A laminated calendar with names of all the stewards. Each month the stewards are reviewed and scored Gold, Silver, or Bronze. The medals are displayed on the calendar, which allows the stewards to see their progress.

Candid Catering A program developed to catalog all digital food images on the banquet and special-events menus. This tool, developed by Chef Carroll, is used in the catering department at River Oaks Country Club (ROCC) for booking banquet parties. Then the appropriate photos are displayed daily on the ROCC kitchen's plasma screen for the culinary team to reference for the day's events.

Certification Product Champion The leadership team member who is responsible for helping and assisting all ROCC culinarians who wish to become certified by the American Culinary Federation. This champion holds meetings with certification candidates and aids them in the process.

Chef & B Chef & Beverage, as in food and beverage manager, the term Chef & B started as chefs in the United States started taking on more responsibilities. Smaller properties might combine the two positions, giving the executive chef the duties of the food and beverage manager.

Chef's Table A chefs' group established by Chef Carroll that meets five times a year strictly for pleasure, friendship, great food, and wine.

CIA (Culinary Institute of America) The school is located in Hyde Park, New York.

Clean and Crisp Award One of the MVC awards given to the culinarian who displays a consistent "Clean and Crisp" appearance every day. See *MVC Award*.

Commitment to Excellence Award One of the MVC awards given to the culinarian who displays the most overall day-to-day dedication to the profession and the River Oaks Country Club Culinary Team. See *MVC Award*.

Culinarians Any person who possesses the desire to work as a professional in the culinary field. A person who shows passion and dedication to and works in the culinary field.

Culinary Certificate Professional certificates complete with a gold ROCC Culinary Team seal and red ribbon. This is a document suitable for framing that the employee receives shortly after starting their employment at the club; it is something tangible they can be proud of. This is yet another sign of our culinary commitment to the employee and his or her importance to the operation.

Culinary Competition Culinary Competitions are held all over the United States. The oldest, largest and most prestigious international culinary competition is the Internationale Kochkunst Ausstellung held every four years in Germany.

Culinary Demonstrations Cooking demonstrations given by a culinarian. A chef who demonstrates different culinary techniques to an audience.

Culinary Mission Statement A summary describing the goals, values, and overall plan of an organization or individual, as it pertains directly to the kitchen.

Culinary Olympics A group of modern international culinary contests involving culinarians. The Culinary Olympics is held every four years in Germany.

Culinary Orientation Package A complete packet explaining all aspects of the culinary program, including the leadership team, incentive programs, mission statement, guiding principles, and awards. This packet is given to all prospective culinary employees.

Culinary Workout Sessions Meetings held every four-to-six weeks including the entire culinary team. This is a mandatory meeting in which guest speakers are invited, culinary demos are performed, new employees are introduced, new policies are presented and explained, gold cards and incentives are awarded, and a "state of the kitchens" address pertaining to food cost and sales are shared with the entire team.

Discipline Any training intended to produce a specific character or pattern of behavior, especially training that produces moral or mental development in a particular direction.

Distinguished Visiting Chef Program A program wherein chefs and culinary teams are invited to stage demonstrations for members and staff, prepare specialty wine dinners, and conduct practice sessions. These visits are very entertaining for members and guests and have proven to be invaluable learning tools for the culinary staff. What better way to inspire your team than to bring an established chef in to showcase his or her talent. This is a great educational tool and benefits everyone.

Educational Environment A thriving culinary educational environment is one where culinary employees are learning on a daily basis. Educational programs include culinary demos and meetings designed to help educate all culinary employees.

Empowering To invest with power, especially legal power or official authority.

Executive Chef The chef in charge of everything related to the kitchen, including menu creation, personnel management, and business aspects.

Executive Sous Chef Second chef; literally, "under chef." The executive sous chef title is usually used in larger operations where there is more than one sous chef.

Exit Interview Given to all employees whose employment with the property is voluntarily terminated. This interview is used as a tool to find out why the employee is leaving and to learn about the employee's experiences in order to make the culinary program stronger.

Family Meal Employee meals. Employee dining.

Garde-Manger An area of a professional kitchen for the preparation and storage of cold foods such as salads, dressings, etc.; the category of foods (also called pantry) and the person who prepares these foods (also called *chef garde-manger, pantry chef*).

Go-Around To go around the table at a leadership team meeting and allow each team member to give a brief five-minute report of any challenges, recommendations or observations he or she has made since the last meeting.

Gold Card The Gold Card Program was established to reward employees for excellence; recognition for those who have gone above and beyond what is expected. An employee who collects three Gold Cards is eligible for selected incentives. Employees who have nominated successful candidates and employees who have received a Gold Card are recognized at the Culinary Workout Sessions.

Gold Standard Part of the Stewarding Calendar of Success, stewards are evaluated every month. Those scoring 85 percent or higher are awarded a gold ROCC Culinary Team emblem. Stewards who average gold for one quarter receive an incentive.

Green Beret Program A program developed at River Oaks Country Club to train, mentor, motivate and prepare eager culinarians in achieving their first executive chef position. These candidates successfully hold all the sous chef positions at the club and culminate their experience by operating the Grill Restaurant. During this program all aspects of River Oaks Country Club are learned.

Guiding Principles A rule or standard, especially of good behavior. The leadership team develops the guiding principles for the culinary team.

Guiding Principle Card A printed and laminated card with the culinary team's guiding principles. It is about the same size as a driver's license;

all ROCC culinary team members are required to carry this card with them at all times.

Guiding Principle of the Week The ideas, values, and beliefs of your operation. The ROCC has twenty guiding principles. Each week, a principle is selected to be the Guiding Principle of the Week, which all team members strive toward.

Human Resources The department and support system responsible for personnel sourcing and hiring, applicant tracking, skills development and tracking, benefits administration, and compliance with associated government regulations.

Incentive Programs A formal program for inducing someone (as employees) to do something. To reward employees for outstanding work ethics with incentives, gifts or recognition.

Inspirational Imparting creative and professional influence on the mind and soul to empower others to move forward in a positive way.

Inspire To affect, guide, or influence others.

Integrity Honesty and virtue.

Job Description The official written description of a position that lists typical tasks, training, education, and experience required or desired, and includes a description of the essential functions to be performed.

Journeyman One who has fully served an apprenticeship in a trade or craft and is a qualified worker in another's employ. A person who has met all the requirements to be certified with the American Culinary Federation.

Leadership The capacity or ability to lead.

Leadership Manual A manual complete with backup material of the culinary team's guiding principles, culinary mission statement, current kitchen policies, procedures, all kitchen programs, and personal notes. It is mandatory for leadership team members to bring the Leadership Manual to all meetings.

Leadership Meeting The scheduled time the leadership team meets. The leadership team meetings are when policies and procedures are developed.

Leadership Team The team within the culinary team that helps the executive chef develop policies, procedures, guiding principles, and a mission statement for the kitchen. The leadership team also helps identify problem areas and develop solutions.

Lighting The devices or techniques used for illumination, usually referring to artificial light sources such as lamps or flashlights. Also contributes to the ambience of the room.

Log Book The daily report of all events and other relevant particulars of a kitchen and attested to by the proper authorities as a true record.

Managers' Meeting A communication meeting held by the general manager, of all the property's managers and department heads. During this meeting all problems, challenges, and possible solutions are discussed as well as future events.

Meeting Minutes An official record of the proceedings of a meeting. Minutes should always be taken at leadership team meetings and previous meeting minutes should always be read at the beginning of leadership team meetings.

Mentor Person who shares experience, knowledge, and wisdom about a particular occupation, their occupation, or about the workplace in general and helps to guide other individuals in the achievement of their goals.

Mentoring Dealing with individuals in terms of their total personality to advise, counsel, or guide them with regard to problems that may be resolved by legal, scientific, clinical, spiritual, or other professional principles.

Menu Challenge To challenge all employees to get involved with the writing of new menus. An effort to get more employees involved and vested in the menu-making process.

Mission Statement A summary describing the goals, values, and overall plan of an organization or individual.

Motivational Something or someone who motivates; an inducement or incentive.

MVC Award (Most Valuable Culinarian) The MVC Award recognizes and rewards excellence among the ROCC Culinary Team members. Once a year up to three employees are recognized for their outstanding work. The recipients are nominated by their peers and receive a certificate, two gold cards, and a trophy.

Newsletter A published document or message, containing news and announcements on a subject.

One-a-Day Meetings Five-minute meetings held every day with each shift. During this meeting, the leadership team member in charge goes over essential information important to the day's events, identifies individual responsibilities, and reviews the guiding principle of the week. One-a-Day Meetings are an important tool of communication.

Passion Strong, enthusiastic devotion to a cause, ideal, or goal and tireless diligence in its furtherance.

Product Champion The individual appointed by the chef to "chair" a new task. The product champion is responsible for developing new concepts and ideas and will champion the new task into reality. Often the product champion will select other culinary team members to serve on ad hoc committees to help in the development stages. The product champion is expected to report progress at every culinary workout session.

Professionalism Award One of the MVC awards given to the culinarian who displays the most positive and consistent attitude of a professional chef.

Program Survival Programs put in place to reassure the survival of other programs. To be sure certain policies and procedure survive and thrive.

Property Tour A tour conducted by three sous chefs given to all prospective culinary employees. It is a complete tour of the entire property.

Purchasing Product Champion The leadership team member who is responsible for researching better products gets more involved with the purchasing software and inventory control and also works as the liaison between the chefs and the purchasing agents.

Recognition and Reward for Excellence Form (RREF Form) A form used to recognize and reward excellence. This form is used by employees to nominate fellow employees for a gold card.

Recognize and Reward Excellence The hallmark of the Gold Card program. Also one of the guiding principles of the ROCC Culinary Team.

Sanitation Inspection Inspection forms developed by the culinary team that reflect the inspection standards of local states' Department of Health. Culinary team members conduct weekly inspections of the kitchens.

Sanitation Product Champion The leadership team member responsible for designing policies and procedures to recommend to the full leadership team that will enhance the overall kitchen sanitation program. This champion leads a team to ensure sanitation and safety standards are met and also schedules inspections of all the kitchens every week.

Saucier The chef in charge of sauces.

SEF Schedule, Empower, Follow Up

Self-Assessment Process in which the learner evaluates his or her level of knowledge and skills.

Sit-Downs A scheduled one-on-one meeting between a member of the culinary team and the executive chef. This meeting is used to get to know the employee a little better and to help define and realize his or her goals.

Sous Chef The chef who is second in authority in a restaurant or kitchen, ranking below the head chef.

Stewarding Evaluation Form A form designed by the Stewarding Product Champion that evaluates each steward's work performance. The scores of this form are logged, and stewards who average a gold standard throughout a calendar quarter receive an incentive.

Stewarding Product Champion The leadership team member who is responsible for designing kitchen-cleaning schedules, helping to develop stewarding-incentive programs, completing monthly evaluation forms, and setting up monthly meetings with the stewards to discuss their performance and challenges and to reward their hard work.

Stewarding Program An incentive program for the stewards that allows the stewards to understand their individual goals, track their work performance, and to receive incentives for good work.

Termination Form A form used when an employee's employment is terminated. This form is used to indicate why the employee is leaving and to make sure that all property items are returned.

Top Gun Award One of the most coveted of the MVC awards. The recipient receives a trophy and a six-week externship experience, all expenses paid. See *MVC Award*.

Vested To place (authority, property, or rights, for example) in the control of a person or group. To give someone an immediate right to present or future possession or enjoyment of their current employment, for example.

Work Ethic A set of values based on the moral virtues of hard work and diligence.

Index